This book was prepared
by CPRS Calgary members,
past and present, as part
of CPRS Calgary's 50th
anniversary celebrations.

Sponsored by
N|A|T|I|O|N|A|L
www.national.ca

$24.95

Barbecues, Booms & Blogs
50 Years of Public Relations in Calgary
Editors: Peter McKenzie-Brown (b. 1947)
             James D. Rennie (b. 1946)

Library and Archives Canada Cataloguing in Publication
McKenzie-Brown, Peter
Barbecues, booms, and blogs : fifty years of public relations in Calgary
/ Peter McKenzie-Brown, James D. Rennie.
ISBN 978-1-55059-363-1
1. Public relations—Alberta—Calgary—History. I. Rennie, James D., 1946-
II. Title.
HD59.6.C3M34 2008   659.2097123'38   C2008-905644-2
Description: On the occasion of the 50th anniversary of the Calgary chapter of the Canadian Public Relations
Society, 18 authors examine various aspects of the practice of public relations in Calgary over the period 1958-2008,
and reflect on the changes that have occurred in terms of how public relations is practiced and perceived.

Design and production by **One Design Inc.**
Calgary

Printed in Canada by **Rhino Print Solutions**
Calgary and Vancouver

RHINO PRINT SOLUTIONS

Detselig Enterprises Ltd.
210, 1220 Kensington Road N.W.
Calgary, Alberta, T2N 3P5
Phone: 403-283-0900
Fax: 403-283-6947
email: temeron@telusplanet.net
www.temerondetselig.com

Support for our publishing program is recognized from the Government
of Canada through the Book Publishing Industry Development Program
(BPIDP). Support is also acknowledged from the **Alberta Foundation for
the Arts** for our publishing program.

Dec 1/08

Kim and Bill

Thought you might be interested part. in ch. 6.

Love

Dad

Barbecues, Booms & Blogs

*50 Years
of Public Relations
in Calgary*

Editors
Peter McKenzie-Brown, APR
Jim Rennie, APR

Table of Contents

Prologue

Peter McKenzie-Brown

Jim Rennie

This project began when Bev Reynolds casually asked Peter McKenzie-Brown whether he would write a history of CPRS Calgary to help celebrate the chapter's 50th anniversary. No money was available, of course, but just *think* of the recognition!

The curious thing is that Peter took the challenge seriously. However, he proposed instead that a variety of experts from within the public relations society each write a chapter. Then, taking a deep breath, he agreed to coordinate such a project.

Working with Henry Stevens' 50th Anniversary Committee, he found support and enthusiasm for the project from many talented individuals. Soon a committee consisting of Don Boynton, Jodi Currie, Jim Rennie and Peter got down to work. Jim agreed to co-chair what we called the Roots Project. Soon after, Leanne Leblanc joined the group.

Although neither of the Co-Chairs is a CPRS member (both left the society a quarter century ago), each has served as chapter President and both are accredited. For all the members of the committee, the significance of this book is that it has captured a history of public relations in this city, and in so doing has captured the history of CPRS Calgary. Its chapters frequently refer to the wisdom, creativity and lives of many men and women who worked in PR. Some were our colleagues; many were (and are) our friends. Their names are in the index.

As we reviewed and edited these chapters, we found the depth of public relations practice in this city—even in the early years—quite striking. We believe the book you are holding in your hands will be instructive for the next generation of PR practitioners.

We hope one particular lesson practitioners will take away from this book is that they are part of a professional community whose roots are not short and shallow, but long and deep. History always involves interplay between flux and continuity, and the story of our profession is no different. In public relations, much has changed, but much more has not.

Peter McKenzie-Brown, APR and Jim Rennie, APR
Co-Chairs, the Roots Project

Foreword

Henry Stevens

I have been extremely fortunate in my public relations career in that I have benefited from access to some of the best minds in the public relations field—individuals who have willingly shared their knowledge with me, and with others. It's worth noting that, frequently, these individuals also share a strong, and often lifelong, commitment to CPRS.

It's not surprising, then, to see many of these individuals represented in the pages of this book, and to see others actively engaged in other aspects of CPRS Calgary's 50th anniversary activities. They have tracked down writers or reviewed individual chapters and made useful suggestions and edits to this book. They have rounded up useful art and artefacts for use in 50th anniversary activities. They have planned and prepared the gala celebration. And they have used networks to find former members and current sponsors. All their contributions are real, valuable and greatly appreciated.

The graphic design and production contributions of Fraser Monaghan and David Stahl of One Design, the quality printing provided by Rhino Print Solutions, the distribution and marketing talents of publisher Ted Giles at Detselig, and the financial support of our sponsor, NATIONAL Public Relations, must also be acknowledged.

Aided by this collective effort, the editors and the other members of what became referred to as the "Roots Project" committee have done an outstanding job of collecting the experiences and perspectives of past, present and future leaders of CPRS and binding them to paper.

The names in the stories and bylines on these pages are a who's who of people who have helped shape and continue to shape CPRS and the practice of public relations here in Calgary and further abroad. This book is a reminder of where we began. It also looks ahead to where we're going and is a very tangible reminder of the importance of CPRS to the development of the field of public relations.

Henry Stevens, APR
Vice-President
NATIONAL Public Relations
Chair, CPRS Calgary 50th Anniversary Committee

A CPRS Calgary backyard barbecue,
circa the late 1970s. Jan Goodwin,
CPRS Calgary President in 1985/86,
is in the foreground.

The Early Years:

Memories of backyard barbecues

By Jim Rennie, APR

Back in the mid-1950s, a small group of Calgary public relations practitioners decided to form an association to share their experiences, ideas and best practices. This is the story of those PR pioneers, how their vision resulted in the formation of CPRS Calgary, and how their leadership set the stage for 50 years of growth and professional development for the society.

One of my first memories of arriving in Calgary in 1954 with my parents was being invited with them to a Grey Cup party at the home of Tommy Steele. Dad was a member of the Imperial Oil public relations team, which meant he had done short stints in Edmonton, then Toronto and then Vancouver, before being transferred to Calgary. For an eight-year-old, that meant the angst of starting over making new friends and getting to know a new city.

That was pretty easy for Dad, since he was always an outgoing sort who made friends easily. It was also easy back then because the city was still pretty small— only about 150,000 people—and the public relations community in Calgary was pretty small (about two dozen) and tended to socialize with each other a lot. They worked for a variety of organizations—government, the agriculture sector, the railway—but the bulk of the public relations community was made up of former newspaper and radio reporters who had been recruited post-Leduc to staff the new public relations positions that were being created by the numerous oil and natural gas companies that were setting up shop in Calgary.

Dad was one such person. Tommy Steele was another—like Dad, he was a former *Edmonton Journal* reporter who had been hired by an oil company (Hudson's Bay Oil and Gas) as their public relations representative. And like Dad, Tommy was an outgoing guy who made friends everywhere he went.

I remember coming away from that Grey Cup day at the Steele household thinking Dad had some fine friends, who were also pretty good to eight-year-olds. I don't remember what the score was that year, but as I recall the Edmonton Eskimos won the cup, and I came away with the proceeds of the modest Grey Cup pool that the members of the Steele and Rennie families had contributed to. A fine introduction to Calgary, to be sure.

At the time, of course, I really wasn't all that interested in what my father did for a living—in fact, it wasn't until years later, when I, too, had entered the public relations field, that I finally started to get a glimmer of what he and his colleagues had been doing.

I hadn't been aware, either, that beginning in 1956 he and his colleagues had begun discussing the formation of a professional association—a Canadian Public Relations Society chapter. Indeed, it wasn't until recently, after reading a handwritten report in the Glenbow Archives about the formation of the society, written by an anonymous CPRS member who had been a part of the planning process, that I really started to fully appreciate those early members as hard-working, visionary professionals.

I knew, of course, that these people all worked with my father. However, I really got to know them only on a very personal level. They were my father's peers,

Past-Presidents from the first 20 years: A commemorative banquet was held at the Palliser Hotel on January 19, 1978, to celebrate 20 years of CPRS Calgary, and to honour past-Presidents. Front row *(left to right)*: Bill Speerstra (1968/69), Cynthia Balfour (1974/76), Gene Zadvorny (1972/73). Middle row: Ken Ford (1958/59), John Neinhuis (1973/74), Brock Hammond (1966/67), John Thorburn (1963/64), John Francis (1964/65), Tom Steele (first President 1957/58), Art Merkel (1969/70), Jim Rennie, Sr. (1959/60), Leo Van Vugt (1977/78). Back row: Bill Ross (a charter member), David Wood (1961/62), David McAsey (1976/77).

but they were also his friends, and many also became my friends. Then some years later, when I joined their ranks professionally, some of them became my colleagues and mentors.

While growing up, a normal day for me would be to come home from school and find Jack and Iris Fleming visiting my parents—Jack was the PR representative for Canadian Western Natural Gas. Or it would be Ken Ford, who was with the City of Calgary. Or I'd be invited with my parents to Jack Balfour's home and end up playing goalie (because I couldn't skate) with Jack's sons on their backyard hockey rink—Jack was a PR representative with Home Oil. Or I'd be "loaned" to David Wood to spend the weekend up at Lake Kananaskis to help him with a cabin he was building—David was with Mannix and went on to create the Public Affairs Bureau for the Alberta Government. Or I'd be invited to go sailing on Glenmore Reservoir with John Thorburn because I was a bit chunky at the time and provided good ballast in a heavy wind—John was with the TransCanada PipeLines PR department.

All of these men played a role in the formation of CPRS Calgary, and all but one served a term as society President. And there were others—Reg Hammond of Royalite, Jim Gray of Home Oil, Bill Ross of Calgary Power and Lorne Frame of Mobil Oil, to name just a few more—who all deserve recognition for their early work with CPRS.

There were also a few, such as John Francis, Calgary's longest serving and much-respected public relations consultant, and Brock Hammond, the PR representative with British American Oil (later Gulf), both of whom I knew while I was growing up, and whom I had the privilege of working for and with a few decades later. They were unusual in that, unlike most of their contemporaries who combined a basic formal education with a news media background, they had impressive academic credentials. John had a Master of Science degree in Public Relations from Boston University, and Brock had both a Master of Arts in Psychology and an MBA from the University of Western Ontario.

One or more university degrees is pretty much a given for entry into public relations today, so in a sense John and Brock were really ahead of their time. But then pretty much everything in the PR toolbox today can trace its roots back to the early days of the society, and those early, enterprising PR practitioners.

One of my strongest memories of those early days is of Dad's backyard barbecues. Dad loved nothing more than inviting friends over for a barbecue, and those friends were as often as not PR people and their families. By the time I was grown and off to university, I knew pretty much the whole Calgary public relations community, without ever really knowing what they did or why they did it. I just knew

Jim Rennie, Sr., one of the charter members of CPRS Calgary, does his best cowboy impersonation riding a stuffed bear in a hotel lobby in Vancouver at the May 1963 CPRS National Conference. A CPRS Calgary delegation brought a bit of the Calgary Stampede with them as part of a pitch to hold the next National Conference in Calgary.

that they loved barbecues, good steaks, and, whenever Dad was involved, the occasional gin.

I didn't know, for example, that Tommy Steele was, as the previously noted anonymous historian put it, "as much the 'father' of Calgary CPRS as anyone." The author was describing a number of gatherings of Calgary PR people in 1956 and 1957 to discuss the creation of a public relations association in the city.

That led to the first formal meeting on April 8, 1957, which saw the election of the first executive, discussion of whether or not to affiliate with the CPRS National Society (which in 1957 included only Montréal, Toronto, Ottawa and B.C.), and the setting of dues. The decision was to join the national body, which required incorporation of the Calgary society, and dues were set at $10 for the local society and $5 for National. Monthly luncheons for the new society were set at $2.25 per person, including one drink, on the last Thursday of the month, at the Palliser Hotel.

Fittingly, Tommy Steele's peers elected him the first President; my father—Jim Rennie, Sr.—and Ken Ford were Vice-Presidents; Bob Wells, of Canadian Husky Oil, was Secretary; and Bill Speerstra, of Shell, was Treasurer. One of the first items of business for the executive was to get the chapter incorporated under The Societies Act of Alberta, and an application dated January 7, 1958, was registered with The Registrar of Joint Stock Companies for the Province of Alberta.

The application was signed by Messrs. Steele, Rennie, Ford, Speerstra and Ross—the charter members of CPRS Calgary.

The society received its Certificate of Incorporation, No. 3006, dated October 16, 1958, and the Calgary chapter of CPRS was in business. Actually, for the first few years it was The Canadian Public Relations Society (Alberta), since the group included a few members from Edmonton.

In the words of our anonymous historian again, the event was noted by a visit from officials from the National Society, which had provided written support for the Calgary application for incorporation. "Jack Brockie was CPRS National President," wrote our historian. "He, and some others, came to Calgary where we held a fine soirée at the Palliser Hotel. We were given our charter, and CPRS Alberta was launched."

When Edmonton moved to form its own society, a quick name change was made, effective February 22, 1962, and The Canadian Public Relations Society, Calgary became an all-Calgary venture.

Women today make up a majority of the membership of CPRS Calgary, and of the total body of practitioners and PR students. But there was really only a handful of skilled and talented women in public relations in Canada 50 years ago, and in Calgary, for the first full year of CPRS operations (1959/60), the society showed a membership roster of 26, all of them men. That, of course, simply reflected the demographics of the business at that time, and soon changed (for the better). By the mid-to-late-1960s, Frances McNab, who ran a consulting business that pre-dated the society, Mary Stemp, Carlotta Blue and Georgia Souter were all members, and running for office in the society. Cynthia Balfour became the local society's first woman President in 1974, and since then, 17 more women have served as President of CPRS Calgary.

CPRS Calgary has always had a social side to it—even professional development events invariably include time to meet, mix and mingle with colleagues. However, I have often thought that my father and his peers probably had more fun doing what they did than subsequent generations of PR people. That isn't to say the first members weren't professionals—they knew how to work hard and party just as hard. But they were extremely competent and innovative communications practitioners who, in many respects, set the stage for pretty much all of the professional developments that practitioners today take for granted.

Right off the bat the members of CPRS Calgary created a strong formal structure, detailed bylaws (14 pages), and a clear sense of purpose. That purpose was the bringing together of those directly engaged in the field of public relations with specific objectives:
- "to advance the art and science of public relations;
- "to maintain high standards in the practice of public relations;
- "to promote and foster discussion on all phases of public relations;
- "to provide a clearing house for ideas and experiences in public relations; and
- "to advance the knowledge, skill and status of those engaged in public relations."

They knew what needed to be done to be a "professional" organization, and they moved quickly to make it happen.

A members' newsletter began appearing regularly in 1961. Relations with the University of Calgary and Mount Royal College were established as early as 1962, as the society began what has been an ongoing objective of CPRS Calgary to assist in the development and delivery of educational programs relating to PR and communications. Also in 1962, a National Education Survey undertaken by CPRS Calgary—initiated and organized by John Francis—was incorporated into the National CPRS report at the annual conference. PR for PR became a working theme for the society. And in 1966 the Calgary chapter strongly endorsed the national plan for member accreditation. Local CPRS programs became less theoretical and more professional-oriented, with guest speakers and resource people—in 1962/63, there was even a Speakers' Bureau, which was the responsibility of Board member Joe Marks of Brown & Root.

On the latter point, I can remember my father telling me about gently chiding another member for suggesting more professional development was needed at the monthly luncheons. Dad, like the other members of the group, was fully aware of the need for all of them to learn and grow professionally. He just wasn't sure it needed to be at the expense of some good drinking time at lunchtime meetings.

The chapter was also keen to make its mark within the national organization, and began campaigning as early as 1960 to hold a National Conference in Calgary. A number of proposals were turned down, and it wasn't until 1968 that Calgary was able to act as host of the first of the four CPRS National Conferences that have been held here.

John Thorburn: CPRS Calgary President in 1963/64, and Chair of the first National Conference held in Calgary, in 1968.

As part of its ongoing efforts to win the right to host a National Conference, in June 1962 John Thorburn was put in charge of the "On to Vancouver" committee, to lead a Calgary delegation to the Vancouver conference held in May 1963 and make a pitch for the next conference. In true Calgary fashion, of course, the conference and the pitch became part of one big party, one that saw a Calgary delegation, and spouses, travel to the conference all together on a train. John Francis remembers it as being "in the true tradition of the Stampede." There was much partying, with a Western flavour, and a young musician who played guitar and sang on the train, and who may or may not have been paid at the end of the trip. Dad recalled someone passing the hat for a young Will Millar, who went on to considerable success with the Irish Rovers. John isn't so sure anyone did remember to pay him.

Although the pitch didn't work out, it was by all accounts a terrific party, and a good conference. And when Calgary finally did get to host a National Conference, in 1968, it was appropriate that John Thorburn should chair it. It was a very successful conference (it set an attendance record and recorded a profit of $4,000), and it was appropriate, I think, that a key social event was a barbecue dinner at the Rafter Six Ranch.

One more CPRS barbecue played an important part in my life. After graduating from university, and marrying the University of Alberta student newspaper editor (Lorraine, the love of my life for more than 40 years), I did a stint at *The Calgary Herald*. Sort of following in my father's footsteps, but still not really knowing what he did for a living.

So when it was time to leave *The Herald*, in the early 1970s, and look for something else, I was invited to one more CPRS Calgary barbecue, to meet some more good people and maybe learn a bit about PR. The party was at Gene Zadvorny's home, Gene being the PR representative at Canadian Western Natural Gas. I had a great time, met some old friends and met some newer CPRS members such as Gene and David Annesley. I also remember the evening as incorporating what looked to me to be every gas company barbecue in southern Alberta. But it wasn't really "educational" in terms of charting my future career moves.

As luck would have it, though, I decided to give PR a try, and landed my first public relations job shortly thereafter. I went to work with Canadian Arctic Gas, the first Mackenzie Valley natural gas pipeline proposal. That gave me the opportunity to work with many of the CPRS people I had known for years. The contacts from the barbecue did help get me to join CPRS Calgary, and then got me nominated to run for office with the society (done, as was typical of the day, without me knowing about it until I saw my name on the ballot) and to eventually serve my own term, in 1979/80 as chapter President.

Unfortunately, I missed the opportunity to work with my father. He retired in 1973 just months before I started. But I did get the opportunity to work with people like John Thorburn, and David Wood, and Brock Hammond, and others, most of whom, sad to say, are no longer with us.

And I very much believe that if they are to be remembered appropriately now, it should be for setting the tone and the standard for the 50 years of achievement and growth that CPRS Calgary is now celebrating. They should be remembered as a fun-loving group of individuals who came together to grow public relations. They were hard-working as well as hard-partying. And they sowed the seeds for pretty much every aspect of public relations specialization that we know today.

Most of them started out primarily doing media relations—and they did it well. Since many of them had media backgrounds, they knew what the media needed and they delivered it professionally and without trying to play games. They worked with their own senior management, briefed them and prepared them for media interviews, years before media training became a specialty. They also developed the concept of media tours—taking working media into the field to see and learn about operations, such as drilling wells in permafrost and building pipelines, and to talk with operations people.

But they also found themselves doing much, much more than just media relations.

Community relations/consultation is an essential regulatory requirement of energy projects today. It got its start 50 years ago with the construction of the first big pipelines and other oil and natural gas projects. It wasn't always pretty or smooth sailing: my father was seconded to Interprovincial Pipe Line when it was built in 1950, and was responsible for keeping communities advised as to what was happening. On one occasion he visited a small community in southern Saskatchewan only to be warmly greeted and then quizzed as to why he was there—the pipeline, after all, had come through three weeks before. Embarrassing experiences like that were part of the learning curve back then, and within a few years Dad and others were effectively establishing and maintaining solid working relationships with key community leaders throughout Western Canada and the North.

Developing good working relationships with local elected officials was part of the process, too, even if government relations wasn't as big a factor as it is today.

The first CPRS Calgary members also volunteered their time and talents for community endeavours such as the Calgary Stampede (Flare Square was just one example) and other civic events. They also helped their employers make worthwhile charitable donation decisions, long before community investment became a specialty.

Financial communications were not as sophisticated as they are now, in the post-Enron era of strict disclosure rules and regulations. But the early society members learned as they went along in this area, too, producing short but necessary annual reports for their companies, and setting down some of the roots that grew into today's investor relations.

In fact, CPRS Calgary was organizing and holding seminars on media relations, government relations and financial relations 30-plus years ago. And even such current growth areas as corporate social responsibility aren't all that new. CPRS Calgary held a CSR conference 28 years ago.

All of us who make or have made our living in public relations owe a very large debt of gratitude to those first members of CPRS Calgary. They may not have had the benefit of computers, email or websites, but they made do with typewriters, telephones, "street smarts" and effective face-to-face communications. They really did sow the seeds for those of us who followed in their footsteps. And if CPRS's roots are strong today—and they are—that is a testimonial to their efforts, their vision—and yes, to their barbecues. They made public relations respectable, professional, and fun.

May the next 50 years be as rewarding.

> *Jim Rennie, APR,* is a native Albertan who came to Calgary in 1954. After graduating with a B.Sc. in Chemistry from the University of Alberta, he worked for five years at *The Calgary Herald*. He then began a 35-year career in public relations, most of it in the energy sector. He worked for Canadian Arctic Gas, the Canadian Petroleum Association, Bralorne Resources, Gulf Canada and FWJ, and retired from Enbridge in December 2007, as Senior Manager, Corporate Communications. He was President of CPRS Calgary in 1979/80.

Cynthia Balfour, President of CPRS Calgary from 1974 to 1976 and first woman on the National Executive, thanks Alberta Premier Peter Lougheed for participating in the 1978 CPRS National Conference held in Calgary.

2

Women in Public Relations:

The first 25 years

By Cynthia Balfour, APR

When CPRS Calgary was formed it was a male-only society. But that changed quickly, and today there are more women in PR, and in CPRS Calgary, than men. In this chapter, two of the first women to stake out senior roles in PR in Calgary discuss their careers and their experiences as "Women in Public Relations".

As I am writing this far from Canada, and years after I was actually involved with women in public relations in Calgary, with no records to fall back on, I find my memory is not as good as I had hoped. It is hard to believe it is 24 years since I left Calgary to return to New Zealand and 36 years since I became a member of the Calgary chapter of CPRS.

The Calgary chapter had been operating for 14 years when I joined in 1972 and at the time there were very few women actually practising PR in the city. Women's roles in PR have changed immensely as have the numbers of women in the profession since then.

I had arrived in Calgary in 1967 and Pat McVean hired me as a copywriter in a very small ad agency. We also did some PR for her clients and I remember organizing some photo shoots at the top of the Calgary Tower (then the Husky Tower), which at the time was under construction. Although Pat would not have regarded herself as a PR person, it was part of her agency service for clients.

After two years with her, I applied for, and got, a job with Francis, Williams & Johnson, the largest PR and advertising agency in Alberta at the time. John Francis, the senior partner, was no chauvinist and was not averse to hiring women as writers and then encouraging them to achieve and progress in their jobs.

As I remember, my title was Industrial Editor. As such, I wrote mainly in-house employee newsletters. At the time, the Calgary Stampede was one of FWJ's main clients and I edited a newsletter called *Saddlebag* for them. My immediate boss, Bill Payne, a CPRS member, entered it in the yearly CPRS competitions and it won first prize in the newsletter section. I suppose this was my first success with CPRS, although I was not a member at the time, and it was satisfying.

I joined the Canadian Industrial Editors Association, which later became Corporate Communicators Canada. There were more women in this organization than in CPRS, since, in most cases, being an "industrial editor" did not include management functions as much as the public relations practitioners' roles did. It seems that, at the time, women joined Corporate Communicators (which became the International Association of Business Communicators) while the guys joined CPRS. However, we did share seminars at times so we all knew each other quite well and were on good terms with them.

At the time, it was pretty much a given that men were better paid than women. In my case, while I was senior to the young, less-experienced man in the next office and was getting $400 a month, he was getting $600, but that was just the way it was. As time went on, women's salaries across the board became more in line with their male counterparts and by the time I retired I was earning an excellent salary and I suspect the other women, particularly in the oil industry, were as well.

In 1972, after about three years with FWJ and with increasing responsibilities including PR activities, and with John's encouragement, I joined CPRS. The company paid our membership fees, which was a help. From the start I enjoyed the professional contacts with people like David McAsey, Leo Van Vugt, David Wood and Gene Zadvorny, soon to be joined by Jan Goodwin, Bev Reynolds and Hope Smith, to name just a few. I also enjoyed the meetings, seminars, friendships and social activities that were all part of being an active member. Once I became a member I quickly moved up the achievement ladder, first passing my accreditation in 1973, and later becoming an examiner myself.

I remember being quite terrified by the thought of sitting an examination, not having done so for at least 25 years! One of the examiners was Sister Ella Zink, APR—a remarkable woman who believed that CPRS accreditation was up to a BA standard, and who was recognized by the National Society for her contributions to public relations by being named the 1976 recipient of the CPRS Award of Attainment. There were two examiners at my accreditation—both impressed me and, what is more, they passed me. For the first time in my life, and in my late 40s, I had academic letters after my name. I'm still proud of that achievement.

In the years that followed, my association with the Calgary chapter, as well as the national organization of which Calgary was a member, increased and I was fortunate to be able to spend time at work on CPRS activities. The first major event was being elected to the Calgary Board of Directors. This led to my being elected President of the Calgary chapter for three years, from 1974 through to

1976, and then being elected President of a short-lived Alberta body comprising the Edmonton and Calgary chapters. In due course I was elected Second Vice-President of the national organization. In every case, I was the first woman to hold the office.

I consider that getting many of the younger Calgary practitioners, both male and female, interested in becoming members of the society was something of an achievement as well. In 1978, I worked on the CPRS National Conference with T.A.G. Watson, one of my early recruits, who chaired the Calgary conference team.

Perhaps because of my own lack of a formal education in this area I was particularly happy to do all I could to encourage and support young women with their own PR careers. By the late 1970s and early 1980s, there were more PR and communications courses being offered by the universities, community colleges and polytechs across Canada and they were becoming very popular with young women.

I was working for Canterra at that time, and I encouraged the company to give two of these women the opportunity to do their work experience programs with us. I had two outstanding young women, over two summers, one from a polytech in Saskatchewan, the other from the recently introduced communications course at Mount Saint Vincent University in Halifax. They were both excellent students, bright, confident and enthusiastic girls who absorbed knowledge like sponges and applied themselves so well to whatever was asked of them. Their colleges had prepared them well and with a minimum of supervision I was able to let them loose on some major projects, such as preparing a video for visitors at the company's sulphur production plant and developing celebratory activities following the completion and opening of a new natural gas pipeline system. Both received congratulations from the company President.

The travel that CPRS entailed included attending board meetings in different cities, and going to national and international conferences. All of which allowed me to meet and get to know other members across Canada and the U.S., as well as to see and get to know more of my adopted country. As a Calgary member, I became involved with the two Calgary colleges, the Southern Alberta Institute of Technology and Mount Royal College. Along with other CPRS members, we were involved directly with both the students and with curriculum development. This was before a Communications degree program was introduced at the University of Calgary and then at Mount Royal. While I was not involved in the latter developments, some CPRS members made major contributions to their introduction. As I recall, most of the first participants were women. Even before that course was introduced, even more young women were looking at the prospects offered in public relations and advertising as chosen careers, rather than as an extension of journalism. At the same time, in the U.S. members were getting worried that PR was becoming a women's profession, that perhaps too many women were breaking through the so-called "glass ceiling".

My own career path had been developing nicely during this time. Following my time with FWJ, I became a partner with Fraser Perry, who had left the world of journalism as Senior Oil Editor of *The Calgary Herald* for the world of public relations, in Resources Communications, a two-person PR firm specializing in resource public relations, principally for the Calgary oilpatch. This was my introduction to a fascinating business area, one that would consume my interest for the next 12 years.

The oil industry was growing very fast with more discoveries of oil and natural gas both locally and worldwide. Calgary was growing with large influxes of professionals from Eastern Canada and overseas, with new oil companies popping up all over the city. It was an exciting time to be involved, but it also exposed me to gender discrimination on a much greater level, this industry being one of the most chauvinistic, as I was quick to find out. For example, the CEO of one of Calgary's major oil companies told my partner not to bother sending me to see him as he would "not deal with a woman." Although I did some work for that company, I never did work directly with him. That was not the general client reaction, thankfully. I developed good working relations with many very senior oilmen. On the whole, I was treated with courtesy and respect, but some middle management men in the last company for which I worked were a bit slower to come round to coping with a woman at their level. Perhaps they felt threatened by a woman!

After the consulting partnership had come to an end, I went to Canadian Arctic Gas and joined a small but talented PR group under Earle Gray, previously Editor of *Oilweek*. The group included Jim Rennie, Dave Smith, Michael Lewis and Tony Stikeman, the latter three working in Toronto. I was fortunate in that I could continue with my CPRS activities, but unfortunately the job did not last long as the consortium was disbanded when it lost the bid to build the Arctic gas pipeline.

My next challenge, both as a PR professional and as a woman in the oilpatch, was interesting because for the first time I really faced sexual discrimination. I was the first PR professional that Aquitaine Canada, a medium-sized French/Canadian oil company had employed and a woman at that. I quickly got the impression that women were few and far between in management in French companies— although several other oil companies had women in their PR departments by this time (1977/78). In the end, I think my professionalism won the day for me, but also my Kiwi "can do" attitude for which we are well known. Particularly, use of good old Kiwi expletives such as "How the bloody hell do you expect me to do my job if you won't tell me anything" helped. Gradually attitudes changed.

I remember going to my first middle management monthly meeting when someone said, "Now we have a woman—she can be the secretary". My reply was I don't mind being the chairman or anything else, but I will not be the secretary. That was probably something of a surprise to them. I had several similar experiences: once, when I wanted some information on a land sale, the landman said, "You are doing your little woman's lib thing, aren't you?" which also elicited a suitable comeback.

The last such incident was in 1984, shortly before I retired to return to New Zealand. It is hard to believe that women were still being subjected to this kind of discrimination at that time. It was at the end of a meeting of several PR people, all men, representing various affiliated out-of-town companies, being held at our office. Both my boss and I attended and at the conclusion one of the men said directly to my boss, Jock Osler, "Would you get 'your girl' to change our return tickets?" My boss was so incensed by that snub that he later demanded they write and apologize to me. I hope they felt duly chastened.

Cynthia Balfour, APR, was born in New Zealand and, in her words, "ended up in PR, not exactly by accident, but by a long series of fortuitous incidents." After stints in advertising in London, and as a writer and editor in New Zealand, she moved to Calgary in 1967 where she worked in public relations as a consultant, and for a number of oil and natural gas companies. She was the first woman to be elected President of CPRS Calgary, in 1974/76, and the first woman on the National Executive, in 1981. She returned to New Zealand in 1984.

Another perspective

By Beverly Reynolds, APR

My involvement with public relations in Calgary began with the Mount Royal College PR program in the early 1970s. There were 20 students in the class, 60 per cent of them male. Only two grads got jobs—both were guys. So I took a job as a secretary in an advertising agency (the same agency where I became Public Relations Vice-President some 13 years later).

I didn't think of this as a male-dominated work-world at the time. That's just the way it was. I was just happy to be working somewhere in the communications industry.

Then I got a job as an Information Services Assistant with a Calgary corporation— TransCanada PipeLines. There were lots of different titles for public relations/public affairs/corporate/reputation management then, just as there are today. During the mid-1970s, ex-journalists, all of them men, staffed corporate PR offices. When I came along, the men were contemplating retirement in the next 10 or so years so companies started looking at hiring additional—younger—staff.

The "new" breed came to the jobs with different backgrounds. Many had associated degrees or diplomas but, again, they were mostly young men. As a young woman, it was a great time to be a member of CPRS.

BAKER LOVICK

CALGARY

Marketing/Advertising/
Public Relations

Beverly Reynolds,   Loic Seheult
APR

R. B. Ranson, General Manager of Baker Lovick Limited, is pleased to announce the appointment of Beverly Reynolds and Loic Seheult to the position of Vice-President.

Beverly Reynolds joined Baker Lovick in 1977 as a PR writer. An accredited member of the Canadian Public Relations Society, Beverly serves on the Board of Directors of the Calgary chapter. She was appointed Senior Public Relations Counsel in 1981 and has made an outstanding contribution in that area.

Beverly Reynolds was one of the first women to reach the senior executive ranks, becoming a Vice-President of Public Relations in 1984.

I was an oddity on the airbus Monday mornings and again on Friday afternoons as I climbed aboard with my briefcase. I worked in Edmonton during sessions of the Alberta Legislature and reported back to the corporation on discussions about natural gas pricing.

As I noted, it was a terrific time to be a woman in PR. I think I got a lot accomplished because I was often the only woman in the meeting or in the complex. Men were courteous, if a little perplexed. For example, while visiting a compressor station in rural Saskatchewan to do a story for the company magazine, I had to ask to use the washroom. Of course there was only one washroom and it had only been used by men. After an initial flurry of activity (clearing the washroom), my needs were accommodated. We all laughed about it later.

In the 1980s, Baker Lovick Advertising made me Public Relations Vice-President. In celebration of this auspicious event, the President of the company flew from Toronto to host a luncheon in my honour. The party of some 12 men (and me) congregated at the Calgary Petroleum Club for lunch. Imagine the surprise when we were told that I couldn't come in! At that time, the Pete Club did not allow women in the main dining room.

Again, a flurry of heated conversation was followed by the "magic" appearance of partitions around the table. The management of the club allowed me to "sneak" in to the table and join my party!

In the early 1990s, I returned to Mount Royal College after being appointed to the Board of Governors. During the six-year term, I was fortunate to be part of the campaign to convince the provincial government to allow the college to have degree-granting status. One of the first applied degrees was in public relations and upon my retirement from the Board I was awarded an honourary degree in Applied Communications (Public Relations).

I am aware that not all women in PR were greeted with open arms, and clearly there were incidents of discrimination. But I had the benefit of strong role models, and in my formative years in public relations it didn't occur to us that our gender would make a difference—and maybe that's why it never held us back from doing what we loved to do.

Beverly M. Reynolds, APR, has worked in public relations in Calgary since the mid-1970s, after graduating from the Mount Royal College public relations program. She worked first in corporate PR with TransCanada PipeLines, and then as a consultant with Baker Lovick Advertising. She continues to provide PR consulting services, as well as community service with agencies such as Inn from the Cold. She is a "Life Member" of CPRS Calgary.

Women in Public Relations:

The present

By the Editors

Cynthia and Beverly were not, of course, the first women in public relations in Calgary. Frances McNab ran her own consulting business before CPRS Calgary was even formed, and although the initial members of CPRS Calgary were all male, by the 1960s women such as Carlotta Blue and Mary Stemp had joined.

And while Cynthia was the first woman President of CPRS Calgary, she certainly wasn't the last. In the 1980s, Jean Flatt (Andryiszyn), Janet Willson and Jan Goodwin served as President of the society. And after that? Since then, 14 different women have served one or more terms as President, with Nancy Arab being the most recent President of CPRS Calgary.

Women have also moved into a definite leadership position in the society. When Cynthia was President, in 1974/76, she was the only woman on the Board. By 1982/83 there were six women Directors on the Board. And in 2007/08, women accounted for eight of the Board members, and all four of the student representatives.

As for membership, it didn't take long for the ranks of women in the society to increase, to the point where women now significantly outnumber men in terms of society membership, the overall PR workforce in Calgary, and the number of students in local PR and communications programs.

Just to give you an idea of the change: in 1959/60, the first full year of CPRS Calgary operations, there were no women members. By the early 1980s there were more than 40 women members, accounting for about one-third of the total membership. And as of June 2008, women accounted for about 70 per cent of the total current and pending members' list.

Today, there are more women than men in CPRS Calgary, and in PR in general in Calgary: women such as Colleen Killingsworth, Gay Robinson and Beth Diamond.

Women's roles in PR have also changed, with more and more women taking senior leadership roles in their organizations. Women like Sheila McIntosh, Executive Vice President for Corporate Communications with EnCana Corporation; Jane Savidant, Vice President and General Manager for Hill & Knowlton Canada in Alberta; Beth Diamond, the Managing Partner of NATIONAL Public Relations; and Pat O'Reilly, Vice President, Communications and Public Affairs at Suncor Energy. There are many others in senior leadership positions throughout the oilpatch, in not-for-profits, in academia, and running their own consulting firms.

As for the future, perhaps a look at the June 2008 student membership list for CPRS Calgary gives an indication—of the 66 student members, almost 86 per cent are women.

Women's participation in PR in general and in CPRS Calgary in particular has changed significantly over the past 50 years. All signs point to it continuing to change, and strengthen, in years to come.

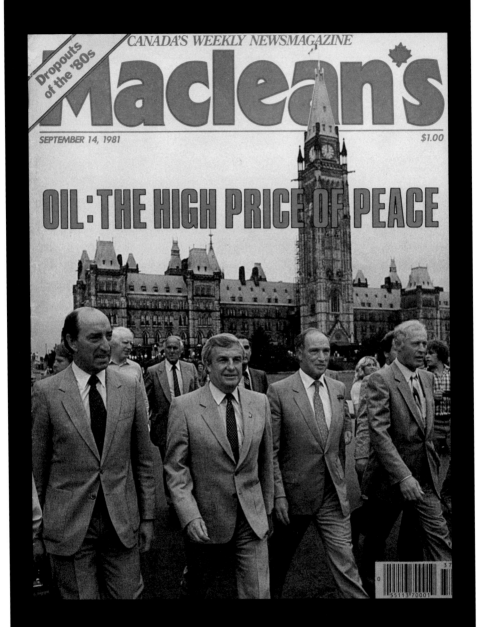

A reflection of the trauma of Canada's energy
wars; cover courtesy *Maclean's Magazine*.
This cover is now a life-size, feature exhibit at
Calgary's Glenbow Museum. (*Left to right*): federal
Energy Minister Marc Lalonde, Alberta Premier
Peter Lougheed, Prime Minister Pierre Trudeau
and Alberta Energy Minister Merv Leitch.

3

Centre of a Storm:

The Canadian Petroleum Association during the energy wars

By Peter McKenzie-Brown, APR

The National Energy Program and the "energy wars" of the late 1970s and early 1980s were a wake-up call for the oil and natural gas industries to start telling their story, to governments, to key interest groups, to the public. The Canadian Petroleum Association led the charge, and a variety of Calgary-based industry associations were created to carry on the communication. This is the story of those emotion-charged times.

The oil price shocks of 1973, 1979/80 and 1986 echoed and re-echoed around the world. Here at home, they aggravated the conflicts that historians now call Canada's energy wars. As the drums of battle deafened public debate and affronted an industry whose allies were few, federal and provincial partisans clashed for petroleum wealth.

Through the Canadian Petroleum Association, oil and gas producers gradually developed a coherent public voice and eventually played a role in policy reform. They also opened their eyes to the critical importance of good environmental practice. This chapter tells those stories.

Energy wars

The battles began with a shot from Prime Minister Pierre Trudeau. Inflation had become a national problem and oil prices were rising, and on September 4, 1973, he asked the western provinces to agree to a voluntary freeze on oil prices. Nine days later, his government imposed a 40-cent tax on every barrel of exported Canadian oil. The tax equalled the difference between domestic and international oil prices, and the revenues were used to subsidize imports for eastern refiners. At a stroke, Ottawa began subsidizing eastern consumers while reducing the revenues available to producing provinces and the petroleum industry.

This outraged Alberta, which had fought long and hard for control of its natural resources. Britain's Privy Council didn't award resource ownership to the province until 1930, after a drawn-out legal battle between Edmonton and Ottawa.

Premier Peter Lougheed soon announced that his government would revise its royalty policy in favour of a system linked to international oil prices. His timing was impeccable. Two days later, on October 6, the Yom Kippur War broke out—a nail-biting affair between Israel and the Arab states. OPEC used the conflict to double the posted price for a barrel of Saudi Arabian light oil, to US$5.14. Saudi Arabia and the other Arab states then imposed embargoes on countries supporting Israel, and oil prices rose quickly to $12.

These events aggravated tensions among provincial and federal leaders. The rest of the 1970s were marked by rapid-fire, escalating moves and counter-moves by Ottawa, western provinces and even Newfoundland. The atmosphere was one of urgency, alarm and crisis, with global conflicts adding gravity to the federal-provincial quarrelling.

Alberta, British Columbia and Saskatchewan (the latter two headed by NDP governments) took steps to increase their revenues from oil and natural gas production and to protect provincial resource ownership from federal encroachment. The federal government announced a series of national policies founded on the basic notions of federal/provincial revenue sharing, made-in-Canada pricing, increasing Canadian ownership of the industry and a quest for self-sufficiency in oil through development of such non-conventional resources as oilsands and the frontiers. [1]

A single voice

The logical voice for the petroleum industry was the Canadian Petroleum Association, a trade association mainly reflecting the interests of large, foreign-owned companies that together produced around 90 per cent of Canada's oil and gas. Formed in 1952, the association's primary function was to compile technical data for the industry—drilling statistics and reserves estimates, for example.

The CPA asserted itself as the industry's voice and quickly found itself in the centre of a storm. Its Executive Director was John Poyen, a capable manager with a technical background. According to Jack Gorman, who later became the association's Director of Public Affairs, "When the feds announced the export tax on oil, from his chair in the CPA office Poyen made some fairly blunt comments, without any reference to the CPA's Board of Governors." Many people in the industry saw Poyen's outburst as a public relations disaster. [2]

Hans Maciej—at that time the association's Technical Director and economist—didn't think so. "John used to call a spade a spade and the feds may not have appreciated his plain talk, but the organization continued to put the industry's case forward." [3]

Harold Millican soon took the top job at the CPA, and Gorman joined him. "It was a happy arrangement," said Gorman. "Our focus at that time was to be conciliatory, especially because of the way Poyen had shaken the beehive and got a lot of people upset. So we developed our messages, and talked about how oil was getting harder to find and told people about different approaches to the problem.

Co-sponsored by:

CANADIAN PETROLEUM ASSOCIATION

and

THE CALGARY PRESS CLUB

Closing date for entries: March 15, 1978

Jim Rennie joined us and we developed an educational approach, producing booklets about the ABCs of the oilpatch."

As an aside, the CPA library became an important centre of PR learning for CPRS members, beginning with Rennie's brief tenure there. Monthly "Library Nights" featured bottles of port and thoughtful discussion about every imaginable aspect of public relations practice. Library Night thrived until 1983, when it reappeared as Shop Talk at another venue. It soon disappeared from the historical record.

"With some difficulty," Gorman continued, "I was able to sell the CPA on a program of journalism awards to get the media to take more interest in our industry. I thought it was also important to hold seminars for reporters and separate seminars for editorial writers. So we brought them into town and set up seminars hosted by experts from the oil industry. It was a warm and credible way of working with the media." [4]

Perhaps, but it was powerless in the face of the worsening political struggles. As Maciej put it, "When politics entered the picture, PR people alone could not play the major role." [5]

The National Energy Program

In 1979/80, further crises in the Middle East led to panic-driven pricing. The Iranian Revolution came first. War between that country and Iraq soon followed. Oil prices more than doubled, to US$36 per barrel.

Such high prices multiplied the amount of money at stake. Pierre Trudeau led the Liberals to electoral victory in 1980, promising vaguely to create a federal energy policy in response to rising oil prices. The result was the National Energy Program, Canada's most controversial federal initiative in peacetime. It ended an era of great prosperity in Alberta.

On October 28, 1980, I worked for Gulf Canada, and that evening I sat glued to the television as the budget speech described the federal government's latest energy initiative. In a beautifully produced book prepared for the occasion by the federal government, Energy Minister Marc Lalonde said, "This is a set of national decisions by the Government of Canada. The decisions relate to energy. They will impinge, however, on almost every sphere of Canadian activity, on the fortunes of every Canadian and on the economic and social structure of the nation for years to come." [6]

Right he was, although no one could have imagined the rancour that followed. A fuming Peter Lougheed compared federal actions to those of a rude invader blundering into Albertans' living rooms. The province made plans to cut oil production by 15 per cent over three months, threatened to withhold approval of new oilsands projects and launched court actions. British Columbia and Saskatchewan mounted furious protests of their own.[7]

The NEP pitted vital interests against each other. Supported by eastern consumers, the federal government took one corner of the ring. Supported by regional voters, the western provinces took the other. The petroleum industry was a spectator wishing it could score points against either combatant—or better, both.

In the beginning, compromise seemed impossible. After a year, however, the two levels of government did reach a revenue-sharing agreement—memorialized in the press by photos of Peter Lougheed and Marc Lalonde toasting the deal with Champagne. Left out in the cold, the petroleum industry didn't share in the celebrations. Under the terms of the new deal, the sector could only realize additional revenue if oil prices, which had already begun to erode, continued to rise.

Operating under new rules in a declining oil price environment, corporate cash flows dropped precipitously. In response to federal efforts to "Canadianize" the sector, foreign interests sold their assets and headed home. The Canadian sector became mired in debt—a development that contributed to the bankruptcy of once-mighty Dome Petroleum. Drilling slid into a deep funk, and rigs began a highly publicized exodus across the border. Confidence in the industry plummeted.

As the decade wore on, bankruptcies in Alberta reached new highs and real estate prices crumbled. Although exacerbated in 1982/83 by what was then the worst global slowdown since the Great Depression, the severity of the decline was unique among the world's petroleum-based economies. Norway, for example, boomed throughout the NEP years.

New leadership

At the beginning of this period, in 1979, the CPA's leadership changed again. Ian Smyth became Executive Director.

Perhaps reflecting his civil service background but with the active support of the CPA's Board, Smyth quickly began to enlarge the association. He began by creating an office in Ottawa to supplement divisional offices in Regina and Victoria.

Before long, the organization also had offices in St. John's, Halifax and Montréal. Smyth's ambitions, and his plans, were vast. "CPA staff often provided access to ministers in Ottawa and the provinces, but we never lobbied in the sense that lobbying is a dirty word," he said. "We'd do show-and-tells. There would be half a dozen ministers around the table, and we would say: 'Here we are, the industry, and we want to tell you what we're doing. If you have any questions, Minister, we will be glad to answer them.' " [8]

Gorman tells a story about this period with a combination of humour and derision: "The next thing you know they hired Allan Gregg, who had just founded Decima Research, to conduct a nationwide survey to find out what Canadians think about the oilpatch. I said to Ian, 'I can tell you what the people of Canada think about the oilpatch. They think it is run by a bunch of Yankee fat cats who are exploiting Canadians and making high profits and sending most of the money back to the U.S.' So they launched their campaign and surveyed Canadians and that's exactly what they found out.

"Then they decided to let the research drive a campaign to convince the Canadian people that this really wasn't true, that the oil industry was really working in the best interests of the country. So they began this big, expensive advertising campaign, but I don't think it was very effective." [9]

Norm Elliott and I joined the CPA in 1981, just before the advertising campaign began. Norm was Director of Public Affairs; I was his number two. Our day-to-day work consisted of analyzing news and planning communications; preparing news releases and backgrounders; organizing news conferences; arranging publicity and media events (including the National Journalism Awards); managing publications, including a monthly magazine and the annual report; speechwriting; meeting and meeting some more. Despite technological innovation and the evolution of new forms of media over the last three decades, these functions are still the PR professional's stock-in-trade. They are less art than craft.

My role gave me a unique vantage point from which to observe the industry's response to the NEP. The balance of this chapter describes how the CPA led the charge.

The leader

Ian Smyth was a big, wall-eyed man with a large ego, a superb mind and, when he turned it on, a huge amount of charm. Few people were able to dominate a social occasion, a meeting or an organization as completely as he did. As Norm Elliott put it, "Ian was the leader. He set the rules, he set the thinking and he knew what was going on. I never saw a better mind than his. It was unbelievable to watch him, to see how people responded to him. He came into Calgary not knowing a soul, and within a year he was right on top of things."

Smyth was a quick study, and his commentary was continual grist for the media's mill. "He could completely take over an interview," said Elliott. "The best media people in the country took him on, but he always controlled the interview. No one could acquire that talent. He was just born with it." [10] Technical Director Hans Maciej continued to answer questions about many economic and most technical matters. On matters of policy, though, Smyth became the industry's spokesman. The CPA was the industry's voice, and he was the CPA's.

When I asked him to describe the advertising campaign, Smyth began thus: "We set out to use opinion polling to find out what concerned people. What we quickly found was that Canadians were not worried about Canada running out of oil. It was a period of high unemployment and high inflation. People wanted to have a job a year from now. That was their number one concern. As we worked through the research, we realized that we had a theme. That theme was that when the petroleum industry is at work and has the funds it needs to do what it does, it provides jobs and employment right across the country. So we began to run a series of TV commercials and print ads telling that story, and it worked."

He added, "That was the most researched campaign in the history of advocacy advertising. It became a case study in some MBA programs. We researched carefully everything we did. If something didn't work we junked it and if it did work we did more of it. And so we gradually progressed to a stage where our campaign had a significant impact on public opinion. Partly because of what we did, voters threw out the Liberal Party in the next election." [11]

Hans Maciej was skeptical about the research, but supported Smyth's conclusion that the campaign helped people understand the damage caused by the NEP. "I always questioned the numbers we were getting back from our advertising and polling people," he said. "We would hear that something in public opinion moved by 0.2 percentage points and that was a major improvement. But Allan (Gregg) was an effective snake oil salesman, and it was always interesting to listen to his interpretations."

"Anyway, I believe we were effective in putting forward the other side while the NEP was collapsing under its own weight," Maciej maintained. "To their credit, the political opposition (Mulroney's Conservatives) saw what was happening. It took them a long time to rectify all the wrongs of the National Energy Program, but they eventually did it." [12]

Emerging issues

Just before the NEP died, the CPA shifted its focus toward the natural environment. The emergence of environmentalism as a public issue illustrates an important rule for the petroleum industry: A crisis for one is often a crisis for many. Take the cornerstone years of 1977 and 1982.

On June 9, 1977, Justice Thomas Berger issued *Northern Frontier, Northern Homeland* [13]—the report of the Mackenzie Valley Pipeline Inquiry, and a surprise bestseller. This document raised environmental and social rather than technical objections to an industrial project. In so doing, it killed a proposal to construct a natural gas pipeline from the Arctic. The industry didn't see this as part of a sea change, but responded with a cacophony of complaints about the "left wingnuts" in Ottawa. Wingnuts or not, 30 years later 1.7 billion barrels of oil and about 25 trillion cubic feet of natural gas remain stranded in the Far North.

Five years on, two calamities struck in a single year. The *Ocean Ranger* disaster off Newfoundland and the Lodgepole blowout in Alberta precipitated more than gripes and grumbles.

The *Ocean Ranger* tragedy involved a semi-submersible drilling rig going down in a winter storm. She took 84 hands into the frigid sea, and none survived. The Lodgepole catastrophe involved an Amoco-operated, high-pressure sour gas well. Out of control for 68 days, it took the lives of two blowout specialists and sent another 16 people to hospital. On days with strong westerly winds, residents of Winnipeg (1,500 kilometres away) could smell the rotten-egg odour of the gas.

Regulatory opprobrium and public anger were intense. Inquiries went on for years, and the resulting new regulations were as tough as nails. More importantly, in Canada's national consciousness these headliners reinforced budding concern about public health, industrial safety and environmental integrity.

The CPA was the first trade association to take action on these growing worries. According to Smyth, this, too, arose from research. "We were continually out there taking the public's pulse. We had noticed from the beginning that the first few top-of-mind issues were always economic—jobs, taxes, inflation and so on. But after a while, people started volunteering the environment as a top-of-mind concern—the only issue

During Stampede 1986, this cartoon by Vance Rodewalt captured the economic collapse in Calgary. *Left to right:* Doug Stoneman, CPA Chairman and Senior Vice-President, Shell Canada; Marcel Masse, federal Energy Minister; Ian Smyth. Source: *The Calgary Herald*, July 9, 1986.

that wasn't bread-and-butter. So I said to the CPA's Board that we should be, and be seen to be, the most environmentally responsible industry in the country, and they said, 'See what you can do.' We began by developing the first industrial environmental code of practice in the country, and soon set up an environmental department." [14]

Third price shock

As the CPA began its environmental labours, the country's energy wars were ending. Then oil prices collapsed, a 1986 market phenomenon known as the third oil price shock. The industry's core issue became survival in a world of lower energy prices.

Environmental policy remained a focus, but big budget ads were suddenly out of the question. The CPA responded with its first and only community relations initiative. With the CBC and *The Calgary Herald* as media sponsors, the association's Share the Earth Triathlon helped brand the CPA green. It was a sporting event with an environmental theme— the first, perhaps, in Calgary.

Why triathlon? It was a new sport and the city (gearing up for the Olympics) was sports mad. The demographics were excellent: a mean age of 36 and surprisingly large cohorts of professionals. Costs were minimal, and volunteers, with leadership from Race Director Pete Strychowskyj, took care of planning and race-day operations. This early-season event quickly became the most popular in Alberta.

The CPA's wisdom in championing the environment became apparent as the Mulroney government began passing tough new environmental legislation. This included million-dollar fines and five-year jail terms for offending executives.

Smyth twice earned honours with *The Globe and Mail's* front-page "Quote of the Day." On the first occasion he said, "I have never seen a CEO who was prepared to trade five years in the slam for a better bottom line." On the other he said, "We have plenty of environmental sticks. We need more carrots." In large part because of the CPA's efforts, Ottawa nominated Canada's petroleum industry to the UN for a prestigious environmental award.

In 1992, the CPA merged with its former shadow—the much smaller Independent Petroleum Association of Canada—to become the Canadian Association of Petroleum Producers (CAPP). The new organization axed the triathlon which, though still popular, had outlived its usefulness.

Legacies

The oil shocks left enduring legacies. One was an increase in industry organizations focused on telling the industry story. For example, the respected Centre for Energy is the successor to the Petroleum Resources Communication Foundation, and the SEEDS (Society, Energy, Environment and Development Studies) Foundation has been producing energy information tools for Canadian schools for more than 30 years.

In addition, companies and trade associations are now far more fluent in government and stakeholder relations than when the CPA's pioneering efforts began. The alphabet soup of industry associations and organizations—CAPP, PSAC, CEPA, CAODC, SEPAC and the rest—are better staffed with or have access to public affairs professionals. They share key messages and backgrounders with their members, so all can respond quickly with the same basic messages. As importantly, senior managers now receive training in how to deal with public issues, and they understand that good environmental performance is the only acceptable business practice.

These developments owe much to the reverberations of the oil price shocks and, later, to the greening of Canada.

Peter McKenzie-Brown, BA, APR, CERTEFL, has worked in the corporate, consulting and academic worlds in Europe, North America and Asia. He began his public relations career with Gulf Canada and worked for the Canadian Petroleum Association prior to developing a writing and consulting practice in the 1990s. He is the author or co-author of four books—three of them on business history. He was President of CPRS Calgary in 1982/83.

Big Oil has explored for and discovered oil and natural gas all across Canada, but the major discoveries have been in Western Canada, off the East Coast, and in the North. This drilling unit—the *Kulluk*—was used by Gulf in the 1980s, and recorded a number of significant discoveries in the Beaufort Sea.

4

Working for Big Oil:

Highs and lows at Dome

By David Annesley, APR

Big Oil has played a big part in Calgary's history, and in the history of CPRS Calgary—a great many of the first society members worked for oil and natural gas companies. This chapter looks back at what it has been like to work in public relations in Big Oil—with the focus on working with the Calgary energy news media, and the fascinating story of Dome Petroleum.

There has seldom been a dull moment in the lives of people who have worked in PR for anything more than seven or eight years. If nothing else, the technology changed sufficiently to keep one on a learning curve. For those of us who are "experience over-achievers", (a.k.a. "old"), the changes have been simply astounding. In the 1960s, for example, simultaneous disclosure for corporations was putting news releases in the mail on the same day, regardless of their destination. That Calgary news media got the release two or more days before the Toronto and other eastern media got it was virtually unavoidable, since the technology did not allow for simultaneous disclosure as we know it today. This led the major media to establish bureaus across Canada and/or to rely on the newspapers' internal entity, Canadian Press, for coverage of stories that were of interest to their readers, viewers or listeners.

For the most part, working in PR for Big Oil companies was not a lot different from working in the same capacity in almost any other organization, with a few notable exceptions that will be discussed later in this epistle. We all had lots of work to do—media relations, employee communications, speechwriting, special events, community relations, etc.—and we faced similar, if not identical, issues such as earning a place in the decision-making of our company/organization or developing ourselves towards a profession through sharing experiences, and education (covered in a chapter of this book by Elaine Dixson, who taught a generation about the PR profession and their craft).

The Canadian Public Relations Society provided a forum for a large number of those initiatives. Your scribe joined CPRS Calgary in 1965 and quickly found an invaluable source of knowledge and experience that could be tapped for the asking.

(Public relations was a male-dominated profession back then and I can only recall two female members, in a total membership of about 40 or 50). Absent much in the way of readily available PR education, a fair percentage of people working in PR in those days were recruited from the media. That still occurs but to a lesser degree, as employers today can hire people with degrees in public relations.

Big Oil

Big Oil in Alberta did not exist until Imperial Oil brought in its first Leduc well on February 13, 1947. There had been previous oil and natural gas discoveries and local uses of those products since the 1880s, when natural gas was discovered near Medicine Hat. Later there were natural gas discoveries at Bow Island (Bow Island gas was pipelined by Canadian Western Natural Gas Company Limited to Calgary in 1912) and in Turner Valley in 1914. Oil was found at Norman Wells, in the Northwest Territories, in 1919 and in the down-dip at Turner Valley in 1936. But the discovery that put Alberta on the world map in terms of energy suppliers definitely was the 1947 Imperial Oil discovery at Leduc.

The discovery enticed other big names to Alberta, some on return visits, many for the first time—Amoco, British Petroleum, Gulf and, more locally, Dome Petroleum and Hudson's Bay Oil and Gas. They joined the firms that had been looking for oil in Alberta for years—Bow Valley, Kaiser, Siebens and Home Oil, to name only a few. These companies either became Big Oil directly, or by being absorbed by others who were successful.

Media and Big Oil PR

As much as we would like to think that the Big Oil PR people were pretty sophisticated, we have to give the media covering Big Oil an equal share of the credit. In fact, they were first off the mark in setting up a forum that ultimately provided more coverage, and more accurate coverage of Big Oil in their various publications and, by extension through Canadian Press, to broadcast media. Their forum was the Canadian Petroleum Writers Association, designed to allow the media to continually upgrade their knowledge of the oil industry. They met every two weeks—more frequently if they could line up oilpatch CEOs with greater frequency. If they could, they worked through the PR person; if not, they would go directly to the CEO.

Sessions involved lunch with the invited executive, followed by an address or presentation and a question period, all of which were entirely off the record (even *The Globe and Mail* agreed that off-the-record meant that none of the discussion was reportable, even on a non-attributed basis). Essentially the sessions were to be treated as backgrounders and were only to provide the media with greater perspective on the oil industry. Should association members wish to follow up later with questions about the subject the executive had discussed, they could, of course, but the executive had every right to simply refuse to answer if that was a sensitive subject for his or her organization. There was never an instance of breaching the off-the-record understanding in the years the Canadian Petroleum Writers Association was active. Reporting improved as well, as members of the association had a much greater understanding of the oil and natural gas business. Relationships between the media and Big Oil PR people were greatly enhanced as a result.[1]

Friends of Friday

Initiated by the public relations people in oilpatch companies and affiliated industry and service organizations, Friends of Friday gatherings are off-the-record as well, but are largely social. They bring together the industry's PR people and the media who cover the oil and natural gas industry over beer and *hors d'oeuvres*, three or four times each year. Not surprisingly, the group meets on Fridays.

Big Oil and the National Energy Program

In another chapter in this book, Peter McKenzie-Brown has described the major challenge facing Big Oil in the industry's history in Alberta and Canada. That was the much-hated National Energy Program. Peter's viewpoint as it was unfolding was that of what was then the Canadian Petroleum Association, now the Canadian Association of Petroleum Producers. The only thing to be added to his description is that the oil companies were conducting government affairs initiatives on their own behalf in addition to the efforts of the industry association.

Dome Petroleum Limited, for example, took its reaction to dazzling heights and with even more dazzling speed. Canada's National Energy Program was revealed in the federal budget speech of October 28, 1980. According to author/journalist Peter Foster, "It was one of the most far-reaching and revolutionary policies ever to have emerged from a Canadian government. It featured hefty new taxes, expropriation of frontier lands, a discriminatory system of grants based on a company's degree of Canadian ownership, and a firm commitment to nationalize a number of foreign-controlled oil companies. It was designed to siphon revenue from Alberta, financially hobble foreign-owned companies and greatly extend government intervention."[2]

"A system of Petroleum Incentive Payments (PIP grants) was to be introduced, direct subsidies for exploration and development depending on the degree of the recipients' Canadian ownership and depending on where the recipient companies were operating, with much higher grants for those operating on federal lands than Alberta lands." [3]

Having established Petro-Canada as a Crown Corporation in 1976, to serve as the federal government's "window to the oil industry" and a force towards more Canadianization of the industry, the government strengthened their presence by awarding Petro-Canada the right to a 25 per cent "back in" on all federal lands, and naming it as the instrument for the acquisition of foreign oil companies. To help fund these initiatives, the federal government added a Canadian Ownership Charge on all gasoline sales, with the proceeds going to Petro-Canada.

Gathered in a boardroom to watch the budget speech, Dome's executives were horrified by what they heard. Not only would they be badly hit by the new taxes, but, since their Canadian ownership was less than 50 per cent, they received only the lowest level of PIP grants. To cap it all, Petro-Canada would be able to walk into 25 per cent of their enormous frontier acreage. [4]

Within days, Dome President Bill Richards came up with a plan to create a new company. It would be controlled by Dome Petroleum but would have the level of Canadian ownership required to qualify for the highest level of PIP grants.

That new company was Dome Canada Limited, to be owned 48 per cent by Dome Petroleum and 52 per cent by Canadian investors through a public offering, which was successfully completed and closed on March 19, 1981. To fund its 48 per cent ownership, Dome put up half of its 48 per cent ownership of TransCanada PipeLines plus a portion of a loan from the Japanese National Oil Company, and paid cash for the number of shares required to complete its ownership obligation.

At virtually the same time, Dome was embarking on the acquisition of Hudson's Bay Oil and Gas, paying more than $2 billion for the majority shareholding owned by Conoco in the U.S., all of it borrowed money. As it turned out, the minority shareholders demanded that the same per share offering be extended to them and a court agreed with them. At the end of the day, Dome had to come up with an additional $2.2 billion, again borrowed.

Sentiments of other oil companies cooled towards Dome, since the formation of Dome Canada was, to them, tacit approval of the National Energy Program. If industry sentiment was "cool" towards Dome, both the industry and public sentiment in Calgary was downright frigid towards Petro-Canada, spawning the disparaging bumper sticker "I'd rather push this thing a mile than buy gas from Petro-Canada." (In 1987 and 1988, Petro-Canada sponsored the Olympic Torch Relay run in support of the Olympic Winter Games in Canada. This was a masterstroke, both in terms of public sentiment towards Petro-Canada and the fact that Petro-Canada became one of the largest retailers of Olympic memorabilia in Canada, and the proceeds that came from their retail success continue to help the Olympic movement.)

Unfortunately, times had changed in Canada's economy and Dome's program of growth through acquisitions had saddled the company with $6.3 billion of debt at a time when interest rates were being pushed as high as 23 per cent.

The banks started to take a more active interest in Dome's affairs when they began to realize that they might not be able to get the debts repaid, especially if oil prices weakened. In late 1982, they insisted that there had to be changes at the most senior levels (i.e. Chairman and CEO Jack Gallagher and President Bill Richards). Further, the Independent Board Committee responsible for recruiting Mr. Gallagher's successor had to get the approval of the banks before the final selection was made.

By the time I arrived at Dome in late August 1983, Mr. Gallagher had left the company, and one of my first duties was to call the media conference at which the departure of Bill Richards was announced. The recruitment team had earlier selected J. Howard Macdonald to succeed Mr. Gallagher, recruiting him from his position of Treasurer of Royal Dutch Shell to become Chairman and CEO of Dome. He arrived on October 1, 1983.

Mr. Macdonald was a master in his ability to delegate, and then let the person he had delegated to do a job, do it. By the end of his first month at Dome, he had become accustomed to coming down the hall to a candy bowl strategically positioned on the counter of a secretarial station outside my office, for a sugar fix. To ensure his daily attendance, I kept the bowl stocked with his favourite candy, wine gums. Armed with a handful of wine gums, Mr. Macdonald would sit in my office and we would chat until his sugar needs were satisfied. I am fairly sure I was the only PR man at the time who had the opportunity to chat with the Chairman and CEO of his organization daily.

One day in late October, Mr. Macdonald asked if he might come to my office later in the day so he could listen to the media calls that would inevitably come in following our quarterly results news release, to be issued when the stock market closed that afternoon. Naturally, I said "yes." (What else do you say to your Chairman and CEO?)

Mr. Macdonald had flown back from London, England, overnight and had come directly to the office from the airport. Thus I knew he was tired and I thought he would listen to an hour or so of the questions, then leave. Being $6.3 billion in debt, we usually got about 80 phone calls from all around the world whenever we issued a news release, particularly a financial one. Because that number of calls means hours on the phone, I used a speakerphone to avoid getting cauliflower ear. When the calls started to come in, Mr. Macdonald was advised and settled into a chair in the corner of my office. Shortly thereafter, I noticed his head was bowed and his eyes were closed, which led me to the false assumption that he had gone to sleep.

An hour and a half into the calls, Alan Bayless, a fine reporter from *The Financial Times of Canada*, who knew the company well, called and asked a number of astute questions, including two to which I did not have adequate answers. I made note of his unanswered questions and advised him I would call him back shortly. My call to the finance department was answered by someone I knew, and I explained briefly who the reporter was and how well he knew the company, then asked the questions. The response was that "We do not give out information at that level of detail." Mr. Macdonald stirred and, addressing the finance department person by his first name, said, "Hi Steve, this is Howard. You know, you're right. We do not give out information at that level of detail normally, but I've been sitting here for the last 90 minutes, listening to how media calls come in and how the answer to one question often gets a follow-up question that gets down into the detail level fairly quickly. I think we're going to have to revisit our policy on what gets used in answering media questions and, in the meantime, I'd appreciate it if you would give David the answer to the questions Alan Bayless asked." He then left my office.

I was left to appease Steve, who I had sandbagged, which cost me a very expensive lunch, but from that day forward I could get virtually any information I needed from anywhere in the company. And the next day, Mr. Macdonald told me that, to a large degree, I was to be the decider of what was discussed in the media and that he felt it was his responsibility to make sure that I was kept so in-the-loop that, if I did make a mistake, it would be a one or two degree off-course error and not 90 degrees.

Stories like that are illustrative of the growth in reliance on public relations to handle difficult, and often-sensitive information on behalf of an organization. This was not restricted to Big Oil, but clearly Big Oil was getting the message.

Dome's final years

So younger readers are not left dangling, let me briefly describe Dome's final few years and its ultimate fate. As already stated, Mr. Macdonald arrived at Dome on October 1, 1983. Wanting to get the problem resolved quickly, he called a meeting of the 54 principal lenders for December 1, 1983, in Calgary, at which he outlined a debt rescheduling program that extended the pay-back period but was doable under the then current $30-to-$35 oil price. The lenders did not buy into the program unanimously, but he implemented the program anyway and everything went smoothly until December 1985 and January 1986. During that period, oil prices slid from $36 to $10 per barrel, a disaster for Dome's cash flow. In May 1986, Dome was forced to announce that it could not make interest payments on its debt.

The situation bumbled along for the rest of the year, with only modest improvement in oil prices. Very quietly, Mr. Macdonald started shopping the company around, hoping that a sale could be arranged that accommodated the shareholders to the extent possible and satisfied the lenders, none of whom would be likely to get 100 cents on the dollar. Bids came in from three parties and Amoco Corporation's bid was selected as the winner. The deal was signed on Good Friday, 1987, but the final negotiations and court proceedings took another 17 months to complete. The merger of Dome Petroleum into Amoco Canada Petroleum Company Limited was closed at precisely noon on September 1, 1988, amid great fanfare. It was a banner moment during an exciting period in our history.

David Annesley, APR, worked in the corporate, government and consulting arenas during his 44-year career in public relations, all of it in Alberta. His first PR job was with Canadian Western Natural Gas Company (now ATCO Gas), which he joined in 1963, and he has worked since in such organizations as James Lovick Limited, Molson's Western Breweries, the Alberta Public Affairs Bureau, Alberta Energy and Natural Resources, Dome Petroleum and TransCanada PipeLines, interspersed with consulting stints at Alberta & Southern Gas and the Canadian Energy Pipeline Association, among others. He was President of CPRS Calgary in 1987/88 and is a "Life Member."

John D. Francis has spent more than 50 years
in public relations in Calgary.

5 Public Relations Consulting:

A commitment to ethical practices and strong client-consultant relationships

By John Francis, APR, FCPRS(H)

John Francis, the dean of Calgary consultants, has been an active member of CPRS Calgary for almost the full 50 years of its existence. In this chapter, John tells the story of the creation of his company, FWJ, and the growth of PR consulting in Calgary. He also shares his insights into the business, his basic rules for successful consulting, and his key lessons learned.

This is a review of public relations consulting in Calgary, written from the experience of the author. It focuses largely on the development of the public relations division of Francis, Williams & Johnson (later FWJ) through the 1950s, 1960s and into the 1970s. I have also included a brief review of the consulting environment in the later years, as seen from my own limited perspective.

This history is heavily biased by my own experience. For many years, my company was the only consultant in the city. Later there were others, but I am unable to write about what they did. Errors of fact, regrettable omissions, names overlooked and viewpoints expressed are entirely my responsibility.

The early days: 1957 to 1967
The first public relations consultant in Calgary was a lady named Frances McNab. I know nothing of her background. She had established a business relationship with one or more Toronto public relations firms in the 1950s. They engaged her to handle the Calgary work for national campaigns that they were handling. Not too long after I started my own business in 1958, she came to me and asked if I would like to take over the work she was doing. I purchased a desk and filing cabinet from her for $50, and she moved on into a different career. I still have the desk. Two of the national clients that I took over from her were the Tea Council of Canada and Canada Savings Bonds for the federal government. Amazingly, I still looked after the CSB assignment well into the 1980s. And I remember (can't get out of my head) the name of the spokeswoman that I took on a media tour for the Tea Council. She was from Ceylon (today's Sri Lanka) and her name was Nirmalene Dasanayake.

The national CSB account was handled for the Bank of Canada by OEB International of Toronto. Lou Cahill was the head of that firm and he had put together a network of PR firms across Canada to handle national accounts. This was the beginning of a wonderful relationship over almost 40 years. Members of the network, called Inside Canada, not only provided services for each other's clients. We also shared experience. This was invaluable to a young upstart who knew virtually nothing about running a consulting business.

Another outstanding Toronto consultant who sent me business and shared experience at CPRS conferences was Charles Tisdall. I fondly remember him taking me to his home in Toronto for dinner, and meeting his twin daughters. Another mentor that I met through CPRS, and who inspired me to believe in myself, was Jack Yocom, who was Gulf Canada's corporate Public Relations Manager.

My first two clients after I had printed letterhead—J.D. Francis & Associates, Public Relations Counsel—were Western Decalta Petroleum and Canadian Export Gas & Oil. I approached each to offer my services in writing and producing their annual report. My fee was $5 per hour.

The relationship with Canadian Export Gas & Oil lasted 21 annual reports and 63 quarterly reports. It ended only when they were bought out. Together we won a first place prize awarded by the New York-based *Financial Times*.

Western Decalta wanted weekly invoices, I guess to keep tabs on me. During the first week I took a professional photographer to Turner Valley to photograph company facilities. My invoice the first week included $30 for my time for this six-hour task. I was called in and asked why it was necessary for me to go along with the photographer. The relationship with Western Decalta lasted one year, at which time they took the annual report in-house. **(Lesson: Clients do not like open-ended billing arrangements.)**

As the business developed, I was able to increase the hourly rate. My profit and loss statement for the year 1961 shows gross income of $19,300, and net profit of $7,468.

How the business grew

When I was just starting out in business, Frank Allison, a colleague of my father, Harry Francis at United Grain Growers, called and asked if I would like to come to a meeting of the new CPRS chapter in Calgary. Of course I was happy to attend and meet the members. Shortly thereafter, my phone rang. It was Jim Rennie, Sr. Jim handled public relations for Imperial Oil. I remember the exact words: he barked, "Are you in business?" Jim was an ex-newspaperman, and sometimes talked like one. After I said "yes", he said that Imperial sponsored the "Teen-Age Safe Driving Roadeo", a competition in which teens drove cars around an obstacle course and demonstrated safe driving skills. He said he had other work on his plate, and would I like to handle the publicity? This was my first publicity effort as a consultant, although I had some experience at my previous job at Calgary Power. It went off successfully, and I earned a fixed fee. I handled the project for a few years until it was discontinued. I've always been grateful to Jim. He didn't see me as a rival, but rather as someone who could help out.

I had been working from home, and began to feel I ought to have an office downtown. A friend had his law practice in the Grain Exchange Building and he suggested I go to see the owner, Harry Mann. He was semi-retired, and retained a marvellous secretary, Betty Nason, who had some spare time. So I moved into a cubicle in his office space, and Betty did my typing, charging $1.40 per hour. In those days, my drafts of annual reports were typed on a manual typewriter using carbon paper to make 10 copies for every meeting with the client management group. This meant every correction had to be erased on every page, and re-typed. Everyone who has done drafts for annual reports knows how tedious this process was.

This office arrangement worked very well from 1960 to 1963, when I decided to hire another professional, and a full-time secretary. I moved into an old warehouse that had been converted to office space—the Cockshutt Building at 12th Avenue and Centre Street South.

The new member of the firm was Douglas G. Evans, a Calgarian who had taken a public relations degree, I believe at Brigham Young in Provo, Utah. Doug had excellent promotional instincts. This was timely, because I had an opportunity to launch the show homes for the new Bel-Aire Estates on Elbow Drive for landowners Harry Cohen, Ted Riback and Norman Green. We put on a major promotion, using old-English branding, antique horse-drawn carriages, and traditional English costumes. With Doug's promotional and advertising skills, we drew 12,000 people at 50 cents each. And Bel-Aire still has a classy reputation 40 years later. Doug went on to head the Alberta Government Travel Bureau, and more recently was teaching at his alma mater.

The move into the Cockshutt Building provided another lift for the firm. A young real estate agent, Gerald Knowlton, looked after leasing space to us. Then he asked me to organize publicity for his announcement that he was acting as agent for the sale of two downtown hotels—the Wales and the Royal—which I did. Then he went out on his own and formed Knowlton Realty, which I wrote the press announcement for. (I also wrote the announcement when he sold the business 30 years later.) Throughout those

30 years, our firm provided him with promotional and public relations assistance on a large number of Calgary office and commercial buildings.

That experience led to many other projects for building owners, from downtown offices to retail malls, to industrial properties.

When I started out, I met Keith Alexander, a recent journalism graduate, who also became a prominent golfer. My marketing brochure showed Keith as an associate of the firm, and it was both of our intentions that he would continue in the business. But he received an attractive offer to go into printing services and sales at *The Calgary Albertan*, a business in which he had an excellent career. Later he became an investment broker in Edmonton. Keith didn't forget me, however. Within that first year of our relationship he was asked to sit on the Calgary Olympic Development Association, which was organizing Calgary's bid for the 1968 Olympic Winter Games. He recommended me to provide services to the committee, and for a while I functioned as their office. A sub-committee was set up in 1959 to produce the "bid-book", and I sat on that with Jay Joffe, a Calgary ad man, and others. We worked as volunteers and produced a fine product. Grenoble, however, was awarded the games. Undaunted, the CODA re-started, and initiated a bid for the 1972 games. I was paid to produce the bid book for this venture. A great effort by dozens of volunteers, supported by a team of professionals, including Lithokraft Press, whose designer, Bob Saunders, did an outstanding job, and writers Jim Rennie and Carlotta Blue. But Sapporo got the games. *(**Lesson: Political power will prevail.**)*

The toughest learning experience was dealing with the loss of capable people, and the loss of clients. Many fine people joined my company, and contributed greatly. I learned that the loss of a good person wasn't all bad—they were frequently replaced by people who brought new capabilities to our clients. Client losses occurred when locally based companies sold out to larger companies, when there were personnel changes, and when we did bad work.

As the company grew, I became familiar with an organization that provided psychological evaluation of candidates for employment and promotion. Gordon Stephenson, a professionally trained psychologist, utilized testing as a tool, and brilliant insights and communication skills in giving me guidance. I was pretty naïve in my ability to read people's capabilities and motivations, and I began to use these services. As a result, our company recruited a number of very capable public relations people in the 1960s. Among them were Carlotta Blue, Owen Lackenbauer, Bill Payne and Frances Dover.

Friends were always my best source of business. In the summer of 1951, my dad got me a job as a timekeeper with Standard Gravel. My supervisor was Bill

Three examples of FWJ's early work. The Travel Alberta Holiday Passport in the late 1970s became Alberta Industry and Tourism's Stamp Around Alberta campaign. The Standard Gravel brochure, created in the early 1960s, was the first of many corporate brochures done by FWJ. The third example, believed to be the first promotional brochure produced by a Calgary PR consultant, was created in 1959 by John Francis: the use of the Thomas Paine quotation about "the irresistible nature of truth" spoke directly to the importance of integrity in PR.

Pratt, a young accountant from Ottawa. We became friends. A few years later—about 1960—he asked me if I could handle a corporate brochure. He had the guts to sell my services to the company's owners, Messrs. Red Dutton and R.F. Jennings, at a time when I was frankly an unknown quantity. I set about getting professional photographs of the company's projects, and writing text. A few months later a prototype was completed, sufficient to show Mr. Jennings. He kept it in his drawer for two years. I think he was waiting until certain projects could be completed so they would look good in photographs. Anyway the brochure took an elapsed time of three years to complete. It was, however, a good product. Later, I was assigned to update it several times, until Standard Gravel became Standard-General, and later part of BACM, and then Genstar. Genstar is long gone, but you still see Standard-General trucks on Calgary streets. The logo on those trucks was designed by Nelson Macdonald, still one of Calgary's most outstanding designers, under my direction. (Nels and I did a lot of work together over the years.)

The Standard Gravel brochure was a good work sample in extending my brochure services to other firms such as consulting engineers, architects and realtors, among others. Outsiders have very little understanding of the complexity of making a corporate brochure. Text must be interesting and persuasive while selecting suitable facts and getting them right; watching the grammar and spelling; commissioning and selecting photography, design and artwork; printing, including selection of paper, ink, colour, and binding; and ordering the best number of copies (make as many as possible to bring down the unit cost, and make as few as possible to avoid stale-dated leftovers).

That summer job, and Bill Pratt's confidence in me, also led to our organizing the grand opening of Heritage Park (Pratt managed the construction of the park) including our Bill Brownridge designing the "H" logo (which disappeared in 2008 with a change in direction at the park); serving the Calgary Stampede (we were already their agency before Pratt went there as General Manager and after he left, but he challenged and inspired us); and the Olympics, where he was President (where we did some of the advance PR , but not the games themselves). (**Lesson: You can't have everything.**)

Another outgrowth of this relationship was that we were engaged to work for Genstar's companies on residential real estate, construction materials and corporate branding.

Openings and other special events are great business for multi-disciplinary firms. Billable tasks include building the invitation list, estimating the attendance, choosing the location, creating a theme, designing the invitation, news coverage, advertising, ordering the catering, tours, chairs and tables, speakers and speeches, WEATHER, ceremony, bar, entertainment, music. We opened Foothills Hospital, a gas plant, a fertilizer plant, Heritage Park, Happy Valley, and countless office buildings and real estate developments. We organized the Treaty Seven Commemoration, attended by Prince Charles, hundreds of Mounties (for security and colour) and news media from the world over. (**Lesson from organizing special events: Attention to detail is primary.**)

One example will suffice. For the Western Co-op Fertilizer plant opening, the guests were arriving, and of course they felt like a cup of coffee before going on a tour of this huge, magnificent facility. The caterer plugged in his coffee machine and somehow shut down the electrical supply for the entire plant. It took two hours to get the coffee.

Corporate brochures and special events are two kinds of work that present a high risk of billing misunderstandings. In an effort to meet all the client's expectations, the consultant will incur considerably more hours of service than the client expects to pay for. Learning this lesson at an early stage, I developed a fee estimating system:

"Our fee will be on an hourly basis not to exceed $___ for the listed service. Disbursements will be estimated separately."

If the client asks for additional services not anticipated at the outset, either some services can be dropped, or the fee increased, with full disclosure to the client. I never minded if we overran our time estimate. We got our quoted fee, and inevitably we got related assignments, and sometimes ongoing business.

Another service that became a mainstay of our PR service was house organs. They provided income every month, or every quarter, and the writing process helped our people become familiar with the goals and needs of the client.

My academic background led me to become an author of public relations master plans. I always wanted clients to be familiar with all the options that a PR professional could deliver. So when we were called in we frequently contracted to prepare a master plan based on a thorough study of the organization and its goals. I persisted in getting the client to identify the organization's publics, and the ways in which each were important. Then I addressed each public, recommending what forms of communications would be most suitable. Quite often we used this process to completely change what the organization was doing, or was considering doing. We often saved them money, reduced their staffing load, and found efficiencies that made their communications more effective.

In addition to the staff members I have already named, we had some real public relations stalwarts who served the firm's clients for long periods of time, and who developed PR business for FWJ. I can't name them all—this would become a list rather than a "bite of history". Some have been introduced in other parts of this chapter.

I must remark on the contribution of Jean Andryiszyn, who provided editorial and journalistic skills as editor of house organs, brochures, and the Calgary Chamber magazine, *Calgary Commerce*. She also developed her skills in news media relations. In latter years she became a specialist in the environmental area, enabling FWJ to offer this service to clients.

It takes a sense of style, coupled with sensitivity to client wishes, to stage a successful special event. Lyn Gilbert was that person at FWJ for many years. Among many outstanding events, she assisted Frances Dover in staging the Treaty Seven Commemoration on behalf of the Blackfoot at Gleichen.

In more recent years, Octavia Malinowski managed special events for us, including a very interesting task related to the '88 Winter Olympics. Octavia and

Judi Gunter organized and ran a hospitality house for a New York bank. World famous guests came to Calgary and stayed for one or two nights at a time, were fed by top chefs, and their every need looked after by the team that FWJ people put together. And the press never found out that these dignitaries were in town.

One of the toughest challenges we faced in the 1950s and 1960s occurred in taking news items to Calgary's most important media organization, *The Calgary Herald*. The City Desk had an attitude that if a story was brought in by anyone other than a reporter (or a whistleblower), it was suspect. And they wouldn't run it! It wasn't just the corporate world that faced these frustrations. While working as a volunteer for community organizations, including the United Way and the Calgary Philharmonic, the treatment was the same. One senior editor was heard to say, "Let them buy ads". They missed a lot of interesting news items.

Radio news, on the other hand, was a great outlet for stories. Calgary had three radio stations (CFCN, CFAC and CKXL) with full-time news departments. They were always interested in what we brought them.

Good public relations practitioners recognize that news organizations make their own decisions about what to say and how to say it; good news organizations recognize that competent PR people, and the organizations they represent, can be a good source of news and features.

When television came along, I tried to take advantage of the face-to-face opportunity that it presented. For our client, the Business Administration division of Mount Royal College, I invented a "case-method" television show called *Decision*. Each week, business executives were invited to participate in a televised round-table discussion of a single business case. The moderator was Chuck Cook, who was Director of the Business Administration program at the college. *Decision* ran on CHCT-TV (now Channel 7) for several years, and Mount Royal College gained significant prestige for its business development program.

Always trying to keep up with client needs, we developed a "media training for executives program" in the 1970s, under Jack Donoghue. Later this became a profit centre for our business when Tom Donoghue, Jack's son, joined us in the 1980s.

A big firm needs financial and administrative stability. This is particularly true of firms that handle large amounts of advertising dollars on behalf of clients. We were fortunate in having Herdin Norgaard, who came to us with Nattall & Maloney, as our Chief Accounting and Financial Officer. He was ably succeeded by Brad Stevens, who ultimately became one of the people who bought me out, together with Nancy Macquade Webb and Tom Donoghue. In the earlier years, Joan Maclagan played an important administrative role, as did Lizz Komar. And

Ruby Choi was a "Rock of Gibraltar", maintaining impeccable accounting records for a long period of time.

Business practices

Very early, I formalized a number of principles of ethical conduct that became integral to the operations of our company, when it was a small PR firm, and later when it was a large PR/advertising/research company. The first was that we would never offer employment to an individual unless he or she contacted us first. The second was that we would never actively solicit business from clients of other PR and advertising companies, unless the prospective client had first asked us for a proposal. When CPRS adopted a code of ethics we embraced it. We never made claims to a client that our service would result in unrealistic benefits.

From my experience, other PR consultants in Calgary followed these practices. Some advertising agencies, however, had a different code. One in particular set out to take away all of our major clients, by discrediting our work, and by offering to make free presentations of creative ideas. In some cases they succeeded. We couldn't retaliate because we had our own code. (**Lesson: Don't assume that your own example of good behaviour will be emulated by others. Most will, but not all.**)

I was always looking for patterns of experience that made the task of running the business more stable and understandable. Over time I developed a couple of formulas, which I had our staff use with clients.

Formula One: You can have any two of the following—low cost, high quality, fast delivery.
a. If you want low cost and high quality, your delivery will take longer.
b. If you want high quality and fast delivery, you will have to pay more.
c. If you want low cost and fast delivery, your quality will suffer.

Formula Two: If you are tendering a job for competition, we are willing to offer any two of the following—we will speculate (do it free), we will do creative work, we will compete with other firms.
a. If you want it free we are willing to show some creative ideas, as long as we are not competing.
b. If you will accept a presentation of credentials, without creative ideas, we will compete without asking for a fee.
c. If you want us to compete, and submit creative ideas, you pay a fee to all competitors.

Other precepts that I lifted from wiser philosophers than I, and preached to my staff, included:

    a. If your project doesn't go as well as you hoped, or you lose the client due to bad work, or misunderstandings, or corporate takeovers, it's all right to be disappointed, but don't get discouraged. When one door closes behind you, another will open before you. In consulting, which relies heavily on project work, it is pretty important to have faith that that door will open.

    b. Make checklists. Break every task up into stages, steps and roles. Designate what the task is, who is to perform it, and when it is to be completed. Use the checklist to monitor progress at regular meetings.

    c. Don't try to do public relations from a distance. PR needs the local knowledge of local professionals—knowledge of the community power structure, the news media, and the culture.

    d. Always make an agreement with the client about fees, and disbursements, before you start. Don't work open-ended and assume you'll be paid.

    e. Know the rules of the business sector of your client. If it's medical, know about medical ethics. If it's investor relations, know the regulations of the stock market. If it's community relations, know the politics.

Education

When CPRS began its accreditation program, I felt obliged to immediately apply, and together with David Wood, successfully completed the first examination process.

When the University of Calgary started its Master's in Communication, Jack Donoghue and I attempted to influence what we saw as a flawed direction. The designers of the program chose a meaning for the word "communication" that we disagreed with. They focused on the technology and laws relating to broadcasting, while public relations focuses on the message, and selecting the appropriate tools of communication. We were unsuccessful, because the department head came from the other side. I've always thought that this was a lost opportunity for Calgary. Fortunately Mount Royal College picked up the slack and developed a fine program that graduated hundreds of students, most with diplomas, but recently with a Bachelor of Communications degree. And the university program has been broadened in recent times.

In 1964 I formed a limited company to own the business. As part of the process a brief history was written, which throws some light on the public relations consulting marketplace at the time. To quote the document:

"The firm has a virtual monopoly on many kinds of public relations services in Alberta. It has outlasted a number of public relations services started by a former mayor, a former managing editor of a daily newspaper, an office opened by a national PR firm, a service offered by a former PR director of the Canadian Petroleum Association, and others. The firm is the only one in Alberta that can undertake opinion research. It handles virtually all local press coverage of national figures who visit Calgary. Plans are being formulated for the opening of an office in Edmonton. The firm has 5 1/2 employees, and occupies 1,500 square feet in a downtown office building."

It is important to note that the success of the firm since its founding was not only due to the active owners and employees. It was, and continued to be, also due to a circle of friends who provided wise counsel and the benefit of their experience. Although not all can be mentioned, I would be remiss in not identifying the people who gave me very important help, both by sending me business, and by helping run the company properly. They start with Lois Francis, who has given me continuing support, made sacrifices, and provided helpful advice for 53 years. They include Douglas Allen, economics and business professional; Fred Christensen, investment entrepreneur; Graham Ross, oil services company owner; William Geddes, Edmonton lawyer; William Tye, senior officer of oil and gas companies; Bill and Joyce Detlefsen, both chartered accountants; Ken Allison and Graham Bennett, both chartered accountants and business executives; Sandy Heard, educator; Ken Manning, true friend; and, very importantly, Jared Paisley, who ably ran our advertising division. I think anyone intending to build a company from scratch is well advised to seek out individuals who have broad business experience that will complement his or her own experience, and who will not hesitate to give sometimes-unpopular advice.

Middle period: late 1960s, 1970s and 1980s

Advertising is often a tool of public relations. And this is where having both capabilities in a firm works to the advantage of the client. The convergence occurs when the public relations requirements call for the purchase of advertising space and airtime—not to sell a brand or a product, but to deliver information and persuade people to the company's point of view. I have always called this "paid space" to get around the idea that corporate people have about sinful and wasteful advertising. Obviously, the word "advertising" has two meanings—the purchase of space, and the delivery of marketing messages. It's valuable to make this distinction in talking to the corporate side. We created many public relations campaigns, some national, that included paid space. Also, of course, public relations is sometimes a servant of advertising, as happens when new products are announced through news events and publicity.

In 1966, with support from some friends, I purchased the Nattall & Maloney advertising agency, located in Calgary and Edmonton, from Harry Nattall. As far as I know, this was the first time in Canada that a PR firm and advertising agency, both well established in their market, came together as equals. From that point on we watched for opportunities to provide both services to clients. As a result, the company grew rapidly throughout the 1970s.

Our growth into advertising meant that my responsibilities were divided, and I spent less time on public relations. At this time, David Wood referred Jack Donoghue to our company.

Jack was a career civil servant who had been one of the most senior public relations officers for the federal government. He retired and moved to Calgary, and I was fortunate to attract him to our firm. He brought to us excellent public relations judgment, maturity, and an understanding of government. He was an outstanding leader of his PR team at our firm. Clients respected him. And I really appreciated many administrative practices he brought to our run-and-gun company. Through his training of staff, and clients, Jack made a difference to the Calgary public relations profession.

While studying public relations at Boston University I became aware of the ways that opinion/attitude research can be utilized in formulating public relations strategy. With this knowledge, I began conducting surveys in the early 1960s. Later I set up Opinion Research Index as a separate division to conduct surveys. We established a "glass curtain" to ensure that the integrity of the research division was not influenced by the clients of the rest of the company. This division, run for many years by Joanne O'Connell, conducted several hundred surveys over a 20-year period, many for clients that were independent of the rest of the agency, and also, where appropriate, surveys for agency clients.

The research division, too, contributed to the growth of the company.

I always thought diversification was good. Looking back, we often were glad we had an Edmonton office, when things were tough in Calgary, and vice versa. We were often glad we had advertising services when public relations was slack. Opinion research contributed a steady flow of income to the pot.

And for a while there was the federal government. In the 1980s we were successful in winning contracts for the federal government, including multiculturalism,

Left to right: Arthur Fiedler, John Francis, and Milt Wright (of Imperial Tobacco, concert sponsor).
Internationally known Boston Pops conductor Arthur Fiedler conducted a number of Calgary Philharmonic
pops concerts in 1970. Wine and champagne were sold to 11,000 audience members over two performances
at the Stampede Corral—the first time the provincial government permitted the sale of alcoholic beverages
at a public event. John conceived and spearheaded the event, which introduced the Philharmonic to a host of
new fans and supporters. He later organized pops concerts conducted by Mitch Miller, with similar success.

youth employment, free trade, and the national census, all of which could just as
easily be termed public relations, although they relied on paid space to deliver the
message. These assignments were not only wonderfully challenging and satisfying to
complete, but they helped see us through the decade.

We implemented a great many public relations/advertising programs,
including "Stamp Around Alberta", which encouraged Albertans to see their own
province by getting passports stamped; Alberta Dairymen's Milk Moustache,
a school-based promotion of milk-drinking directed at teens; Calgary Airport
Authority branding; the application of A-Channel for licensing in Calgary and
Edmonton; creation and editing of a monthly business magazine for the Calgary
Chamber of Commerce; the Petroleum Resources Communication Foundation's
national campaign to inform Canadians about the energy industry; and Save
Canada, a campaign to fight the National Energy Program.

We also contributed our professional time to further the goals of a number
of charitable and cultural institutions in Calgary. Some of those where we "made
a difference" include the Calgary Philharmonic, Alberta Theatre Projects and the

Parks Foundation (all of which I served as President), Strathcona Tweedsmuir School, Glenbow Museum, Devonian Foundation, the United Way, the Calgary Winter Festival and the World Figure Skating Championships.

The consulting marketplace

We weren't alone. More and more firms came into the market starting in the 1970s and 1980s, and increasingly in the 1990s. Some of the people involved moved on to other things and some are still active in the business. All of them advanced our profession through their client work and through their contribution of skills and time to worthwhile community organizations.

They include firms such as Public & Industrial Relations, Baker Lovick Advertising and McVean Advertising. And they include individuals such as Fraser Perry and Cynthia Balfour, who partnered back in the early 1970s, Jock Osler, Jared Joynt, Beverly Reynolds, Paul Clark, Ralph Brinsmead, Gordon McCann, Maureen Payne, David McAsey, and Pat and Sheridan McVean.

They also experienced the ups and downs of doing business in Alberta, just as we did at Francis, Williams & Johnson.

The 1970s had been a dynamic boom period for the economy, and for our company and other consultants and marketing communicators. We had big challenges and opportunities. Our greatest problem was a shortage of trained people. As fast as we trained them, they moved on to more senior positions in companies and government.

The 1980s were just as brutal as the 1970s were prosperous. We went through four devastating recessions. The first was the Trudeau-Lalonde National Energy Program, which hammered our economy, beginning in 1981. The immediate impact of the NEP was to force all of us in the consulting business to lay off staff, renegotiate office leases, and cut expenses in many other ways.

At the same time, governments on both sides of the border instigated tight money to get inflation (interest rates were 18 per cent) under control, which meant that clients reduced spending.

In the mid-1980s came a recession caused by low oil prices, with the result that many small local energy clients were bought out by big companies.

And late in the 1980s came the introduction of computer technology. This meant a decade-long downward adjustment to staffing, and costly investments in technology for our firms. We all had to adjust to computerized graphic design, and to word processing. That period, which was capped off by the Alberta government slashing communications budgets in the mid-1990s, lasted until the turn of the century.

A number of fresh consultants nevertheless ventured out on their own, perhaps for the same reason I did in the 1950s (the economy was so flat that I couldn't get a job in PR, even though I had a newly minted Master's degree).

Some of them—including quite a few FWJ alumni—did very well in the profession. People such as Tom Donoghue, Beth Diamond, Judi Gunter, Jim Osborne, Glenna Cross, Jamie Huxley, Gay Robinson and Lisa Homer.

The consulting business today is certainly bigger than it was even a few decades ago, and it comes in a variety of different sizes, shapes and configurations.

There are the big full-service firms, most of them national or international, with a solid presence in Calgary. This group includes NATIONAL Public Relations, Hill & Knowlton, Weber Shandwick and Fleishman-Hillard.

There are also a lot of smaller consulting firms, most offering a variety of services but usually with a major area of specialization, such as public consultation, investor relations or government relations. This would include firms such as McVean Communications, Brookline Public Relations, Cross Wise Communications, Communica Public Affairs, Concentric Public Affairs and Henderson Communications.

There are numerous one-person shops now, too, many of which extend the range of their services by creating alliances with others—and creating entities such as Donoghue & Associates (Tom Donoghue has become one of North America's leading specialists in media training), Judi Gunter & Associates and Gerry Kruk & Associates. This "associates" approach enables consultants today to provide a wide range of services while keeping the overhead down—something all consultants quickly learn is a necessity.

And finally, there is a relatively recent development of freelance professionals who work alone and work from home. Actually, freelancers have always existed in the consulting business, but what is new is the proliferation of home-based consultants and the very strong market in Calgary for their services. This group includes parents who prefer working at home to be with their families; the growing number of public relations professionals who are retiring but still want to keep their hand in the game; and others who just prefer the home atmosphere to downtown office work.

This growth in home-based consulting has been made possible in large part by computerization, and the ability to keep in touch with clients electronically on a 24/7 basis. To the extent that this approach reduces the face-time in meetings with clients, I think it's a negative: I believe it is very difficult to assess the goals and the culture of client organizations without considerable face-to-face contact.

I do, however, appreciate the speed and efficiency that the computer affords, and as long as consultants are still able to maintain sufficient personal contact with clients, I think the home-based approach can be a welcome addition to consulting.

It is just another change in a business that has changed dramatically in the past 50 years, and will likely continue to change. The only constant for success then and now is the need for a strong consultant-client working relationship.

Conclusion

I have attempted in this chapter to present a picture of public relations consulting in Calgary beginning in 1958, and running through a rather quiet period of learning and experience in the 1960s, the boom of the 1970s, the bust of the 1980s, and maturity and transition into new ways of doing business today.

Looking at a promotional brochure we published in the mid-1970s, I ran across a paragraph that pretty much epitomizes what we were about, and what I would hope still represents the attitude of today's consultants:

"Our job is to reach people. Through honest, creative, factual advertising we reach people to tell your story or sell your product. Through accurate, intelligent, well-planned public relations programs we reach people to change or reinforce attitudes. In our daily contact with clients, the media, the suppliers, the public, we reach people on a friendly, honourable, businesslike basis".

John Francis, APR, FCPRS(H), was born and educated in Calgary, and has lived his entire life here. He earned a Bachelor of Commerce degree at the University of Alberta in 1953, and then entered the public relations field as Assistant to the Director of Public Relations at Calgary Power (now TransAlta). In 1956/58 he took a Master of Science program at Boston University, earning his degree in Public Relations upon completion of a Master's thesis entitled *Public Relations Problems of American Petroleum Companies in Canada.* In 1958 he founded what ultimately became FWJ Communications, a public relations, advertising and research company with offices in Calgary and Edmonton. He sold the company to senior staff in 1996. He continues to provide professional advisory services, primarily through MKM, an Edmonton-based marketing agency. He was President of CPRS Calgary in 1964/65, and is a "Life Member."

A CASE STUDY: Fish Creek Park public participation

In late 1973, Premier Peter Lougheed appointed Calgary architect William Milne to chair a committee to find out what kind of a park Calgarians wanted to create at Fish Creek Provincial Park, on land recently acquired by the government. Milne's committee engaged John Francis and his company, Francis, Williams & Johnson, to provide communications services.

The agency's public relations people helped the committee make media statements before, during and after the public participation program. Its advertising group used paid space to articulate, and repeat, the committee's requests for participation. John's research company, Opinion Research Index, also designed a survey, with carefully balanced questions, illustrated with cartoons by Nelson Macdonald.

John recommended that the survey go to as much of the population as possible, rather than the usual practice of taking a random sample. A postage-paid, self-reply questionnaire was distributed to the entire circulation (165,000) of *The Calgary Herald* and *The Calgary Albertan*, to garner opinions and ideas for the design of what became Alberta's largest provincial park within the boundaries of a city.

John remembers assuring the committee that they would get 5,000 to 10,000 replies—then praying that he was right. They actually got 31,700. It was overwhelming. The committee completed its report to the government, results were reported back to Calgarians using news stories and full-page ads, and the end result was that the provincial government received a clear political mandate for the design of the park.

The Olympic Torch Relay enters Calgary for the XV Olympic Winter Games in 1988, with Premier Peter Lougheed front and centre. The torch relay was "an undertaking of national proportions with unequalled enthusiastic public support."

6

XV Olympic Winter Games:

Leading up to the global limelight

By J.G. (Jerry) Joynt, APR

Organizing and running the XV Olympic Winter Games in 1988 was a major undertaking for Calgarians—one done on the world stage. And a major part of it all involved public relations—coping with the media, the politics, the seemingly endless issues that had to be addressed, and finally, the reward of knowing you have succeeded in putting on what was described as "the best games ever."

In these few pages, I will attempt to give you a taste of the public relations opportunities, challenges and results we faced during the run-up to the Olympic Winter Games—particularly during the three and a half years before the opening ceremonies held on February 13, 1988. The International Olympic Committee (IOC) awarded Calgary the games in Baden-Baden, Germany in the fall of 1981. Bilingual (the official languages of the IOC are French and English), the bid committee in its transformation to the Organizing Committee Olympic Games (OCOG) wisely adopted the bilingual acronym OCO '88—for "Olympiques Calgary Olympics".

The symbol of the Calgary games was a stylized snowflake and a maple leaf; the designer deliberately made it ambiguous. The body of this image consists of five sets of double Cs, for "Calgary, Canada." Hidden within the design are five pairs of cowboy boots. The design uses the red colour from the Canadian and Calgary flags. We always combined this symbol with the five-ring logo of the IOC.

Setting the stage

It would be impossible in the space allotted to cover all the activities of the communications group (shown in detail at the end of this chapter) as all activities have some PR connotations. Instead, I will offer detail in three areas that affected us during the pre-games period. These are media relations, the Calgary Olympic Centre, and the Olympic Torch Relay.

OCO '88 was probably the last organizing committee to have almost total control of the games with tacit approval from the IOC. We ran the torch relay fully, contracted all sponsors, including the big guys, contracted the host broadcaster and wrote contracts with national and international TV networks. Perhaps most importantly, we got paid first, then sent IOC their share.

That is no longer the case. The host broadcaster is now a Spanish company (odd that that is where former IOC President Juan Antonio Samaranch comes from). All the major sponsors are now part of the TOP (Total Olympic Program), which is arranged by the IOC, and all network TV licences are arranged by the IOC. In addition, the IOC sold the rights to the Olympic Torch Relay to Coca-Cola, so who knows who now has the ultimate authority on the route and other issues.

The sport of politics

Although I'm obviously biased, I feel the Calgary Olympics were "the best games ever," as Mr. Samaranch said at the time. The reason for this boast is that, to my knowledge—and with the exception of Los Angeles in 1984—no other games have shown a surplus large enough to leave a legacy to maintain the facilities they required. The Calgary Olympic Development Association is custodian to a number of OCO funds. With the principal held in perpetuity, the endowment subsidizes Canada Olympic Park, the University of Calgary Speed Skating Oval, the Canmore Nordic Centre and many athletic programs. If you go through the history of other games, you will find excessive over-expenditures and, in many cases, grandiose facilities that are not used or have become white elephants.

Most of us think of the Olympic Games as the foremost sporting event in the world of multi-sport events. Except for the games themselves, however, the Olympics and the activities surrounding them are about politics, pure and simple. Special interest groups, opposition politicians, countries with international quarrels and virtually anyone with a longstanding complaint with society or government—all these groups and more use the Olympic Games as a wagon to carry their message.

The most odious case was the 1936 games, which Hitler used to showcase "Arian supremacy." And during this year's Olympiad, the Tibetan issue and China's human rights record did not play out well for Beijing. Homelessness and eastside poverty and other social issues are already in play for Vancouver in 2010.

Calgary '88 had its own political protest. The Lubicon Lake Indian Nation took the political limelight by arguing that they had been trying to get a reserve for a century. They tried to sabotage the "As the Spirit Sings" artefact display at the Glenbow Museum—an important cultural event sponsored by Shell during our games. At Prince's Island Park, a supporter of the Lubicon threw a snowball at former Premier Peter Lougheed during the torch relay, and Peter promptly handed me the torch. Other than that we had few problems.

The spirit

The Olympic Games definitely helped increase front-of-mind awareness of the city of Calgary, and it increased tourism. However, in our travels of the northern hemisphere many people already knew of Calgary through Banff, the Rocky Mountains and last but not least the Calgary Stampede. They were also aware of our Western image, and although some of our Calgary sophisticates thought wearing white cowboy hats, Western-cut clothes and boots was hokey, visitors from Europe, Asia, Great Britain and the Soviet Union sure didn't feel that way! Also, our mascot program was tremendously successful—polar bears Heidi and Howdy were the last Olympic mascots that were huggable, fun and well understood by the public.

Calgarians will discuss the legacy of the games for many years to come. However, one factor that is not in dispute is the tremendous support that Calgary, surrounding towns and villages and rural areas offered.

The volunteer spirit at that time was a showcase to the world of what people with passionate beliefs can achieve. We had 10,000 registered volunteers working during the games and 9,000 unregistered volunteers took part in the opening and closing ceremonies. The number of staff peaked at 501 a year before the games began, and we used 200 consultants and part-time advisors. Probably tens of thousands of volunteers assisted Petro-Canada and OCO '88 with the Olympic Torch Relay, which used vehicles supplied by General Motors.

By the time the games were over, there were no doubters about Calgary's goodwill and "we'll get it done with a handshake" attitude.

Calgary established many firsts. We increased the length of the Winter Games to 16 days from 12. We had a covered speed skating oval and the longest continual torch relay. We made extensive use of volunteers, had the largest TV contract in history (ABC TV paid US$309 million), the highest Olympic flame on top of the Calgary Tower, permanent Olympic flame cauldrons at all venues (still in use), and individual media village bedrooms with phones. We even had an official licensed candlemaker, who cashed in on the torch relay and closing ceremonies.

Media relations

Had it not been for tremendous public support and our great crew of volunteers, we might have suffered Denver's fate with the media negativity that surrounded us. OCO '88 CEO Frank King once said to me, "Jerry isn't it great that everybody recognizes us and waves? Do you suppose that once the games are over they will use all their fingers?"

Jerry Joynt at a news conference in the Calgary Olympic Centre media theatre: once the COC was opened and OCO '88 had a "storefront" for the public to visit, negative comments about the games dropped significantly.

I believe we did everything possible to work up front with the media and be accessible at all times, but one of the media outlets had as their Olympic writer a journalist who had lived through the Montréal Olympics and had a natural suspicion about everything we said. Until about three months before the games started, we faced accusations of overspending, incompetence and, after a ticket scandal, dishonesty.

During 1985 and 1986, every news conference, every event—virtually everything we did—was under intense public and media scrutiny, and almost always received negative coverage. The absolute low came in October/November 1986. It started with a false high, when on our first day of mail-in applications of ticket sales we received 54,000 requests—the largest first-day ticket request in Olympic history. It was all downhill from there.

To begin with, the Lubicons nationally announced their intention to sabotage the efforts of the Glenbow Museum to gathering artefacts from around the world for the "As the World Sings" exhibit, which was a cornerstone of the Olympic Arts Festival. Then the ethnic community went to Mayor Ralph Klein with the complaint that they were not formally involved, particularly in the Arts Festival. Shortly thereafter, the chiefs of the Treaty Six Nations in southern Alberta demanded recognition of some sort in the Olympic Games. And then, in an interview with *The Globe and Mail*, our Arts Festival Manager called the Festival Committee's Chair—a respected professional in the arts community—a "volunteer housewife."

Up to that point we had been feeding raw hamburger to the media. Now we laid out sirloin steak. This took the form of the arrest and subsequent charges for fraud of our Ticket Manager, Jim McGregor. He had developed a ticket sales scam, perpetrated mainly in the U.S. After the games he was found guilty and went to jail for two years, but he caused almost irreparable damage to our reputation.

Those six weeks had me virtually afraid to review newspaper, radio and TV coverage. I had to continually tell Frank King, Bill Pratt and the rest of our gang not to read, watch or listen to the media with high scrutiny, because the public doesn't do that anyway. I received four death threats by telephone at home. They came late at night—fueled by liquid courage, I suspect. Our security force identified three of the callers and paid visits to them. The fourth was never found.

The public could understand and even accept without rancour media charges of incompetence. However, allegations of dishonesty were outside the pale. It took us a long time and a change in game plan to regain public confidence.

The change in game plan came early in 1987. We formed a Communications Review Committee with Frank King, who became a full-time employee as Chairman and Chief Executive Officer, serving the role of spokesman. He met weekly with Mayor Ralph Klein, his assistant Rod Love, Gary Arthur (Frank's Executive Assistant) and Renée Smith, who represented our Information Services Division. These meetings covered such topics as public positioning.

At about the same time, our biggest nemesis in the media got a new assignment. A young journalist who was far more prone to give credit where it was due replaced him. This journalist stayed on the Olympic file until well past the games. He is now a highly respected columnist on the national scene.

The Calgary Olympic Centre

Negative public opinion was a major headache for OCO '88. It was evident through phone-in shows, letters to the editor and forum-type meetings. The common criticisms were that we were inaccessible, that we met behind closed doors like an old boys' club, and that our constituents (everyone) didn't really interest us.

In 1984, under Fording Coal's leadership, the Canadian Pacific Enterprises companies came together with a proposal to become a sponsor of the XV Olympic Winter Games. We negotiated their sponsorship of the Calgary Olympic Centre, which would be located at the base of the Calgary Tower. At the time, that building was CP property.

The COC, which opened in 1986, was probably one of the best PR moves that we could have made. It had interpretive exhibits in a display area for the public. It had a board/meeting room for associated groups, a reception area for entertainment of special guests, and perhaps most importantly a 100-seat media/presentation theatre. All OCO '88 news conferences took place there. You would be surprised how much more comfortable it is to have these events on your own turf. From the time we opened the general public area—run by uniformed volunteers and open

Volunteers and staff assemble to work at the main media centre.

12 hours a day at no cost to OCO '88—negative comments and letters to the editor dropped by 80 per cent. We finally had a storefront.

The pubic interpretive centre consisted of a 50-seat theatre, with an eight-minute, 35-projector slide show with sound and music. This opened into an area where you could ask questions on computer screens, go for a virtual bobsleigh ride, or ski jump or get involved in a hockey game. That was more than 20 years ago: imagine what you could do with today's technology!

Both Frank King and I have suggested to VANOC that they create an Olympic Centre like the one CP created at the bottom of the tower. At this writing, they haven't done it, and they are being accused of being secretive and inaccessible. History seems to be repeating itself.

The positives begin

Things really turned around about six months before the games and continued until they were over. Our relationship with the media had improved to the point we were almost buddies.

CTV was the official broadcaster, the official host broadcaster (paid by us to supply the total signal to the international broadcast centre) and the rights holder in Canada to broadcast the games. As partners, they were a little easier on us, but the competition on who could be the most negative was tough due to the (low) standard set by the aforementioned journalist.

In 1985, Ken King and Bob Poole of *The Calgary Sun*, and Patrick O'Callahan and Kevin Peterson of *The Calgary Herald*, approached us. Each wanted to become the official newspaper. After much soul-searching and discussions with my colleagues on the management team, we decided there would be no official newspaper. In hindsight, that may have been a mistake: had we chosen *The Calgary Herald* we could have neutered our old nemesis like a steer in the back 40.

Jerry Joynt *(left)* and Gene Zadvorny of Canadian Western Natural Gas at the announcement that CWNG would build and supply natural gas for the Calgary Tower cauldron and venue cauldrons, for the Olympic flame. *Above,* a helicopter lowers the cauldron to the top of the Calgary Tower, in November 1987.

Eventually we made the decision and agreed with long-time friend, journalist and weekly newspaper publisher Jack Tennant and his group to publish *Calgary '88.* It was a monthly publication distributed to all homes in Calgary and surrounding areas. We supplied story ideas but did not do the writing. The sale of advertising paid for the activity, provided a profit to the publisher and cost OCO '88 nothing.

Vancouver does not face this problem, as they are essentially a one-newspaper town. *The Vancouver Sun* is already a partner with the Vancouver Olympic Committee (VANOC), and a January 2008 story on the official opening of the sliding venue near Whistler deserves mention. The headline read "State of the Art Sliding Venue Opens Early and On Budget." Yet in paragraph 15 the article briefly mentioned that the original budget was $54 million while the actual cost was twice that amount. If such a thing had happened here I can barely imagine what the headlines would have been, and how many heads would have rolled in response to the resulting political and public pressure.

Olympic Torch Relay

In late 1985, two corporations approached us about taking on sponsorship of the Olympic Torch Relay. They were TransCanada Telephone System, which at that time consisted of the provincial Crown Corporation telephone companies, and Petro-Canada, then a relative newcomer to Calgary and the federal government's Crown Corporation in the petroleum industry. We entered into a contract with Petro-Canada primarily because it meant we would be dealing with a single company headquartered in Calgary but with operations throughout Canada.

During our negotiations with Petro-Canada, we agreed that they would look after most of the organization and staffing, including dedicating appropriate staff across the country to coordinate activities. The responsibility of OCO '88 was to supply an active participant to their staff. We hired Jim Hunter—a noted Crazy Canuck skier—to work with them. The approval process rested with my office.

A decision was made that more than 95 per cent of the kilometres would be available through a lottery. This gave all Canadians the possibility of participating in the torch relay. In February 1987, 10 million torchbearer application forms went out, reaching virtually every Canadian household. This nationwide lottery helped spread the Olympic spirit, generating countrywide enthusiasm for the Calgary games. From nearly seven million entries, 6,520 Canadians were chosen and added to a special selection list that included Olympians, mentally/physically challenged, Aboriginal Canadians and a scattering of the good and the great.

The route began in St John's, Newfoundland, and the relay began on November 17, 1987. It travelled down many secondary roads and through the capitals of every province plus Yellowknife, Whitehorse and Inuvik. The total distance was 18 000 kilometres. A convoy of 80 people and 40 support vehicles travelled with the torch at an average of 125 kilometres a day. The route was within a two-hour drive of 90 per cent of the Canadian population.

Much more could be written on the torch relay and has through various books. It would be reasonable to say that the unique Olympic torch in the shape of the Calgary Tower and the torch relay itself was an undertaking of national proportions with unequalled enthusiastic public impact.

Ed Lakusta—at the time President of Petro-Canada—said the relay was the finest thing his company had ever done. Even sceptics began to believe Petro-Canada had a place in the oilpatch, and its gasoline sales soared.

Compare our experience to the torch relay for Beijing 2008. Yes, it was an amazing thing to take the flame up Mount Everest, and the organizers did much else that should be acknowledged. But by taking the flame to countries and places where the organizers could have no control, the event became more than a PR disaster that tarnished the Beijing games. It contaminated the spirit of the Olympic flame itself. That, perhaps, represents a loss to us all.

Conclusion

I have offered only an overview of the role PR played during this important moment in Calgary's history. To give you a better idea of how extensive our PR efforts were, I have summarized below the public affairs functions of the XV Olympic Winter Games.

Culture: The Olympic Arts Festival; opening and closing ceremonies; venue ceremonies; native programs; Athletes' Village entertainment; medals; Olympic Plaza ceremonies; recognition ceremonies; visual arts; Mask; Olympax '88; billboard; Art Exhibition; Literary Arts; cauldron lighting ceremonies.

Media: Media relations (local, national and international); preparation of all information materials in both official Olympic languages; translation services; on-venue language services (24 languages); main press centre planning and operations; Media Village liaison; coordination of logistics for media—transportation, accreditation and so on; venue press centres; photo pools; and liaison with host broadcaster and rights holders.

Public Relations: Olympic Torch Relay; Olympic school and youth programs; production of Olympic materials for media; pageantry; production and advertising; community relations; liaison with ethnic groups; mascot program; speakers bureau; Olympians program; venue tours; promotions; public meetings; Calgary Tower Olympic Flame; Calgary Olympic Centre; approval of Olympic symbol use; official final report; and official film.

Jerry Joynt, APR, began his public relations career in 1960 in Regina, following graduation from Luther College. He was President of CPRS Regina in the early 1970s, at which time he also received his accreditation. Since moving to Calgary in 1975 he has held senior communications/PR roles in the corporate, agency, consultancy, and government sectors. An active volunteer, he has also held senior PR positions in industry associations, not-for-profits, and special event organizations. Jerry was a member of the XV Olympic Winter Games Organizing Committee's executive management team responsible for the Culture, Media, and Public Relations Divisions. He was a member of the International Olympic Committee Press Commission until 1991.

Press conferences used to attract hordes of radio, television and print media: now they're media conferences, and the event has to be something special to draw a crowd like this.

7

PR and Media:

Hacks and flacks

By Tom Donoghue, APR

Media relations has always been a cornerstone of what public relations is all about. Have the news media and PR people changed over 50 years? And has the working relationship between the two changed? Two Calgary veterans who have worked in both camps offer their perspectives.

They're a bunch of truth-distorting, sensationalizing bastards who just want to sell papers and boost ratings.

They're nothing but flacks, spin doctors and liars who want free publicity for their companies.

We've all heard it before. It could have been spoken in the 1950s, or yesterday, usually by non-PR people or self-righteous journalists, but sometimes by skilled PR professionals and knowledgeable journalists, but said with a smile and a twinkle in the eye.

Fifty years ago, the media appreciated honest, timely information from PR people and PR people appreciated fair and accurate reporting. The same is true today.

There are many examples of loose-cannon reporters who don't deserve the time of day, but there are still far too many PR people who think they can make the media do what they want, or who are ready to stonewall and earn the contempt of good reporters.

The fact the annual standing-room-only Hacks and Flacks Christmas party thrived for years in Calgary shows the media and PR community can and do get along just fine. We each have a job to do and if we respect the other's needs we all win.

Fifty years ago the working relationship was simpler because most PR people came from newsrooms. They had a better first-hand understanding of what the reporters and editors needed. While today's PR person and the reporter are better educated, they often have more theory than practical experience, or sometimes common sense.

Fifty years ago these two communities met at the Calgary Press Club. Press clubs were places where reporters and editors could buy affordable beer and food because salaries were low. A starting reporter in the late 1950s and 1960s might make $50 per week before taxes. Restaurants and country clubs were out.

You had arrived if you made $10,000 a year. Many reporters abandoned the newsroom for handsome PR salaries.

The Calgary Press Club was a somewhat seedy spot to sit over a beer with local media. Cost of membership was cheap. Drinks were cheap. Food was sometimes questionable, but Stampede Week was fun.

Sometimes reporters would try to get inside information about a company from PR sources, or PR people would work at getting to know reporters better and build relationships.

The PR crowd had Petroleum Club memberships. PR bought lunch and the drinks. The all-afternoon "five-martini lunch" really did exist. In the 1970s and 1980s the media became concerned about the optics and insisted they pay their own way.

Now, some senior media have Pete Club and other memberships and take the PR crowd out, since fewer PR people now have these perks.

The Press Club was the birthplace of the Oilweek Annual Report Awards when the PR community and the media came together and suggested its first terms of reference.

The Calgary Herald's move from downtown to Deerfoot Trail in the 1970s, plus escalating media salaries, marked the end of the club.

In the 1970s, CBC radio and television had a big news staff. When covering a major event, you could count on reporters from CBC's local, provincial, regional and national units to show up, and that was just radio.

Television crews included reporters and camera operators from each level. Sometimes they'd have their own grips. If you were hoping CBC would stick around, you needed LOTS of sandwiches.

Then came the shift in terminology from "press" to "news". A Calgary television news director refused to send crews to news conferences if the errant PR person referred to a press release, or a press conference.

He'd say you obviously only wanted print media attending. We learned. Today it's news releases and news conferences. His point stuck.

There was a time when a certain reporter for a national media outlet would do an interview and, if the story was complex, the reporter would send the story to the PR person for checking. On one occasion the PR type sent the story to his company President for verification.

Unfortunately, rather than contacting his corporate PR person about errors in the yet unpublished piece, the President called the paper directly. The reporter didn't lose his/her job, but it was close. That relationship of trust was over.

Fifty years ago, free booze in media rooms, or at events where media were invited, was normal. PR people became bartenders and most media just sucked it back. The news stories may not have improved, but it sure helped media attendance at events.

In the past 50 years, two earth-shaking events fundamentally changed the nature and character of both the PR and news media communities—Watergate and the Internet.

Before Watergate, journalists were "ink-stained wretches" who made little money, lived in a nether underworld, were driven by a higher calling to get the story, get it right, get it first, get it out, to fight for the little guy and drink far too much alcohol doing it.

With Watergate—one of English-language journalism's most extraordinary examples of relentless, digging, researching, fact checking, source cultivating, in-the-trenches journalism—reporters became celebrities. Salaries soared. Already inflated egos ballooned to galactic proportions. Enrolment in journalism schools exploded.

Advocacy journalism replaced objective journalism. Reporters became cause-driven crusaders. The public's silent, grudging admiration was replaced by increasingly deep suspicion, distrust and disdain that continue to this day.

For the PR community, the Internet transformed the universe. Vast amounts of information could be made available and distributed at the speed of light. Websites replaced media kits. Search engines replaced phone calls and visits to the *Herald's* and *Sun's* morgues.

The Internet permanently altered the way the PR community and the news media interact and serve the public.

Reporters use websites for information and participate in online conference calls. But they still want to get the interview with, and quote from, the CEO.

One now-retired PR guy tells the story of a Calgary business reporter who would contact him via email while both listened to the company earnings conference call. The reporter would email questions while senior management spoke on the call and our colleague would fire back answers.

When it was all over, the reporter would call to set up a short one-on-one interview with the CEO; all very efficient.

The Internet has delivered a downside. Young journalists and their slightly older editors are almost illiterate. Despite the computer's Spell Check, they still can't spell, haven't the faintest idea about grammar and obviously don't bother to proofread copy.

There is hardly a story that doesn't have one or more grammatical and/or spelling errors, sometimes in the headline. For the computer and text-messaging generation it may not be important. But the public sees the sloppiness and doesn't take the story seriously. If reporters can't get the basics of their craft correct, why should we have faith in the content and ideas in the story?

Fifty years ago the copy might not have been so colourful, or clever, but it was well written, well proofed and therefore more believable. Editors were fanatical about grammar, spelling, CP style, crystal-clear writing and linguistic detail, and enforced the rules from the top of their lungs.

The volume of information now available because of the Internet was unimaginable 50 years ago. We are connected to the world and each other like never before.

The media is the message. Volume has replaced substance. Tools are more important than content. Professionalism is out. Amateurism is in.

The public used to get information about the world and the community from trained, experienced, full-time professional reporters and editors.

The Internet has delivered Citizen Journalism where anyone with a computer can click and publish stream-of-consciousness thoughts, blogs, photos, poems, opinions, shaky, blurry, jerky, amateur video and what they had for breakfast and present it as journalism.

There's a lot of junk out there whose content may be mildly entertaining, but is it reliable, accurate, provable, valuable, useful and enlightening? The virtual journalism universe has become "homemovies.com" making professionally trained and experienced reporters and editors more valuable than ever.

In the virtual world, the importance of the good old-fashioned relationship between the professional PR community and the professional news is unchanged, but in many ways more valuable and necessary.

As PR people, we must still simplify messages for our companies and clients and deliver open, honest, reliable, accurate and publicly relevant information to the news media for their consideration.

Just like 50 years ago, Calgary's reporters and editors know the idiots in their ranks. They still encounter PR amateurs, manipulators, self-serving time wasters, annoying sycophants and bullying executives.

But they also know Calgary's true PR professionals who understand deadlines, return phone calls, keep promises, and give reliable, accurate, timely, publicly relevant information from their companies and clients.

They also know when the PR professional is caught in the middle, when some primitive-minded executive demands the company sell the media a turkey, a non-story, a fluff piece of spin and empty self-serving propaganda.

Just like 50 years ago, the PR professional still gets a charge when contacting the cave dwelling executive to say the "pitch" was met with a sneering voice at the end of the phone saying, "Buy an ad."

No free lunch

By Judi Gunter, APR

In 1984, the outspoken and often controversial *Calgary Herald* columnist Catherine Ford spoke to CPRS members about the relationship between PR and the media. Her topic? "Since when does a free lunch warrant a full-page spread?"

Her talk was aimed at the publicists, press agents and information officers among us who were expected to get "good ink" for our organizations. Our bosses and clients assumed we could just pick up the phone and get a story placed on the front page, call our friends in the media or just "shop it around." Catherine and her colleagues pejoratively called us spin doctors and flacks.

While the people doing this job 25 years later call their work "media relations" it's quite possible that nothing Catherine had to say then would be different today, except perhaps those free lunches and other sorts of perquisites, junkets and gifts we once needed to have in our toolbox are now anathema.

What has not changed over the years is that to get a story placed we still need to "connect the dots" between what matters to our audiences and how what we have to add to the public record is relevant or interesting or compelling. And true. We still need to develop the right angle and pitch it to the right reporter at the right time and in the right way.

We still need to "facilitate" by providing background and perspective on our industries and our organizations to help media to ask the right questions. No thanks to voice mail and telephone tag though! It's still our job to make our experts

The authors of this chapter—Tom Donoghue *(second from left)* and Judi Gunter *(front centre)*—first met at the 1984 CPRS Calgary Town Crier Awards. Other award winners that year were *(left to right)* John Francis, Larry Jensen, and Tim Finnis. Derrick Pieters *(second from right)*, from the Edmonton chapter of CPRS, was a judge for the Calgary awards.

ready, willing, able and accessible to take their questions. We're still challenged to conjure up that picture that tells a thousand words.

Communications technology and the Internet have also forced media relations practitioners to pick up their pace. We used to hustle to meet media deadlines for tomorrow's edition, the top of the hour or the six o'clock news. Today's deadlines are "right now" since reporters need to get the story on the web immediately. The quicker we can respond, the more control we can have over the message. Tomorrow is too late.

Many of the PR practitioners who are nudging retirement now came into the business from the media 30 or 40 years ago. We are leaving the field with war stories and fond memories and shaking our heads at how much the tools have changed. We remember the leap from manual typewriters and carbon paper to Selectrics and whiteout, from walking the news release over to putting it "on the wire". Fax has come and gone and the World Wide Web has spun off Web 2.0.

Most of us did get up to speed on the "information highway" but we have less time and energy now to take the high-speed learning curve into the brave new world of social media. We're giving way to the generation that blogs and podcasts and hobnobs with reporters on Facebook.

The game is now being played on both the media and PR sides by college- and university-trained professionals who learned their craft—often side by side— in state-of-the-art facilities. Armed with our respective codes of ethics, we should see ourselves as allies in a war on web-based misinformation.

Thanks to media convergence, the trend is towards PR enjoying an increasingly productive relationship with journalists who gather and report the news across the media spectrum including radio, TV, print and the web.

Could today's media relations professionals, serving up good stories in an electronic buffet of information to feed the multi-media maw, fire back an answer to that question Catherine posed a quarter century ago?

Duh. Whatever.

Tom Donoghue, APR, and **Judi Gunter, APR**, probably first crossed trails in 1971 as "ink-stained wretches" working at rival Winnipeg dailies, the *Tribune* and the *Free Press* respectively. The first time they remember meeting, though, they shared the Town Crier Award winners circle in 1984. In the late 1980s they worked together at FWJ Communications. They married in 1993.

Tom has been President of Donoghue & Associates Inc. since 2000 and is a partner in Worldcom Public Relations Group and a member of the Public Relations Society of America. Judi has been President of Judi Gunter & Associates since 1990. She was President of CPRS Calgary in 1990/91 and 1999/2000, and is a "Life Member."

Fifty years ago there were no public relations courses available in Calgary. Now the city has three post-secondary institutions offering a variety of certificate, undergraduate degree and graduate degree programs in public relations and communications.

8

Town Meets Gown:

The role of CPRS Calgary in public relations education

By Elaine Dixson, APR

Professional development, and the desire to see Calgary post-secondary educational institutions provide more and better formal education specifically for public relations, have been priorities for CPRS Calgary throughout the society's 50 years. In this chapter, a Calgary PR professional who has been a leader in the development and delivery of some of those programs takes a look at courses, content and issues in the city, and the role CPRS has played.

Do you realize how badly we public relations people want to be *real professionals*? Just like the doctors and lawyers to whom we continually compare ourselves? We've been pining for recognition as a profession practically since the days of American consultants Edward Bernays and Ivy Lee in the early decades of the 20th Century, roughly 70 or 75 years ago. No other goal has captured our collective interest the way becoming a recognized profession has. It endures as a topic of discussion at our conferences and professional development events, and its pursuit also lies at the heart of how public relations education has evolved in every country in the world. By virtue of the type of institution in which educational programs reside, the way in which they are designed, the content that is taught, and who teaches, all represent an articulation of some aspect of the quest for professional status, and that includes the three-four-five-six (count them!) very different courses and programs that have developed at the Southern Alberta Institute of Technology, Mount Royal College and the University of Calgary.

The quest for credentials

Particularly in the 1920s and 1930s, Bernays and Lee advanced the role of the public relations counsellor who worked directly with the senior leadership of an organization, and who therefore was in a position of greatest influence. Their work demonstrated the critical importance of *being at the management table* if public relations was to be of maximum value to the organization and its work. Naturally, the personal credibility of the practitioner at the management table also had something to do with the leadership's willingness to accept his or her advice. Initially, sheer force of personality was possibly enough of a qualification to earn the respect of management, but by the mid-1930s and 1940s, public relations practitioners found themselves at the management table with recent graduates from schools of engineering, accounting, law, and the newly-recognized social sciences. These were the days when public relations practice was largely focused around media relations or promotions, where years spent at a typewriter as a reporter was considered preparation enough.

Nevertheless, practitioners felt the erosion of their credibility as advisors to management as those around them professionalized. Their dilemma was that there were no public relations programs available to them, although it is true that schools of journalism were opening, few though these were. Interestingly, the perceived need to hold a relevant credential of some kind in order to legitimize one's position at the management table is the reason why the newly-established Public Relations Society of America (PRSA) developed its accreditation program. The specific intention was to put in place a professional industry-developed and managed credential that would effectively level the boardroom playing field for practitioners counselling management. When Canadian practitioners established the Canadian Public Relations Society (CPRS) a few years later, as PRSA's sister organization, we also adopted the accreditation program as a way of quickly putting in place a credentialing program to serve Canadian practitioners in the same way and for the same purpose.

The quest for professionalization

Even as the accreditation programs were being developed in the 1950s, only the most innocent of practitioners could have believed that an accreditation credential would last as a proxy for an academic degree, and so while the accreditation programs continued to grow, individuals or small groups of practitioners, with or without the support of CPRS chapters, sought to establish public relations programs at their local post-secondary institutions.

Several things need to be said about the context in which these efforts took place in order to appreciate why the public relations educational landscape is what it is in Canada. The desire to establish public relations education in academic institutions was in no way intended to denigrate or undermine the value of the accreditation program, although to be sure, there were those who probably doubted the likelihood of the accreditation program surviving if the professional credential had to compete with an academic degree. The desire to establish public relations courses at academic institutions actually was grounded in a growing desire for public relations to gain status as a recognized profession.

Public relations was hardly the only field interested in professionalizing. Particularly in the 1940s, universities that had traditionally accepted their role in preparing individuals for the professions such as medicine and law began opening schools of architecture, education, business and even journalism—heretical developments to traditional academics who did not view these as professions, but merely as fields or occupations. As such, they had no business being housed at universities. The arguments at the time generated a fairly active discussion around the question of "What is a profession?"

One of the seminal responses to this question is Peter Wright's,[1] who in 1951 described a profession as, "a self-selected, self-disciplined group of individuals who hold themselves out to the public as possessing a special skill derived from education and training and who are prepared to exercise that skill primarily in the interests of others." This notion of exercising one's skill in the interests of others, or "in the public interest" as this idea has since been reinterpreted, was a hallmark of the early principled practitioners such as Bernays, Lee, and others. Because they had articulated that public relations ought to be practiced in the public interest, this position was accepted as proof for the argument that public relations had met one of the tests for being recognized as a profession. The thinking was that if public relations could conceivably meet this criterion of being a profession, perhaps it could meet the others as well. Indeed, it came to be understood that "self-selection" referred to "membership" in a professional organization such as PRSA or CPRS, and such organizations were understood to be the "self-disciplined groups" referred to, and which would assume the role and responsibility for governing and regulating the practice of their professional members.

The only thing left to work out, then, was the issue of the "special skill derived from education and training". The accreditation process having been recognized as inadequate to meet this test, we turned our attention to our local colleges and universities.

Establishing the first program

Where should public relations be taught? In the 1950s and 1960s, when the concerted effort to establish public relations programs in Calgary began in earnest, the question was moot. The Calgary branch of the University of Alberta began offering courses in the 1940s, but did not have autonomy in decision-making until passage of the Universities Act in 1966, the effect of which was to create the University of Calgary. Meanwhile, Mount Royal College had been established since 1910, and the Southern Alberta Institute of Technology (SAIT) since 1916. In other centres (in Western Canada in particular), the story was much the same: community colleges or trade schools tended to predate universities, so the fact of the matter was that they were the only game in town. In Eastern Canada, a number of universities certainly had long and rich histories by this time, but like their American counterparts, they also held the entrenched view that training for "non-professions" did not necessarily belong at universities.

It would take almost 20 years before the question as to where public relations should be taught would become relevant in the industry in Calgary. In the meantime, the Calgary chapter of CPRS succeeded in negotiating the establishment of a part-time diploma program at Mount Royal College in the mid-1960s. The program included courses in writing, media relations, advertising and promotions, and yes, even ethics was a topic in the curriculum. The instructors were some of Calgary's best working professionals whose day-to-day experiences provided right-to-the-minute case examples for their courses.

Early program growth and development

One of the instructors at Mount Royal was decidedly not the role model that so many of the others were, and his penchant for becoming too familiar with female students eventually escalated beyond his mere removal from the classroom to his membership in CPRS being challenged by the local CPRS chapter on grounds that his behaviour constituted a breach of the CPRS Code of Ethics. Disputes over Code of Ethics violations were rare, and this case constituted a test of the code and of the national organization that had members across the country watching with interest.

The case went to discovery in the offices of a Calgary legal firm, with the chapter, CPRS National and the person being investigated represented by counsel. Before the hearing could begin, the lawyer for the accused noted that the national organization had only given his client 29 days notice, rather than the 30 days called for in the CPRS by-laws. The hearing, therefore, could not proceed, and the chapter was faced with the option of continuing this expensive and time-consuming process or simply dropping the case. It chose the latter. Several respected members of the public relations community withdrew their own memberships from CPRS in protest.

There was a decidedly negative impact on the credibility of the public relations program at Mount Royal College as a result. When I began to teach in the program in 1984 I still felt the reverberations. I admit to having paid little attention to the program before I joined the college. I was certainly aware of its existence, but during those early years of my own career and relative newness as a CPRS member, I had no particular cause to learn about it. However, when I began to tell colleagues that I had accepted the teaching position in the program, I was rather surprised to discover that the mention of the program was greeted variously with blank stares, smirks of contempt, alarm, and sometimes outright hostility. What can of worms had I just opened, I wondered?

I am sometimes credited with having started the public relations program at Mount Royal College. It isn't true. The program began as a series of part-time evening courses that then became a part-time diploma, and then in 1980 a two-year full-time diploma with a single full-time faculty member to teach the courses and co-ordinate the administration of it. The first full-time faculty member left mid-way through the first semester. The second full-time faculty member was Yvonne Adam, APR, who had practiced at SAIT and at the Calgary Exhibition and Stampede. In her three years with the program, she took the fledgling diploma program and put it on track. She created a stable program that was gaining support in a number of quarters in the professional community. I took it as my responsibility to build on her work.

Who should teach public relations?

I have mentioned the college's somewhat calamitous experience with instructional staff in order to demonstrate the relevance of what some treat as one of those tediously arcane questions that are the purview of academics: who should teach public relations? This question—along with the others I have used to structure this piece—is one of the central themes explored in the public relations literature relating to academic development in our field. Mount Royal College's experience shows just how very fragile our few programs are, how their success or failure is utterly dependent on the skills, knowledge, and experience of whoever leads them, and then, how very vulnerable they are to any limitations of those qualities in the instructors.

Consider this fact: at the time I applied for the position at Mount Royal College, I had eight years of public relations experience, I possessed a Bachelor of Journalism degree, and had begun the course work in the Master of Communications Studies program at the University of Calgary. When I had been on the job for a year or so, I learned from one of my colleagues in the Communications Department that my "competition" for the position had included a used-car salesman from Brooks who claimed he "knew everything about PR" and two local radio personalities who had proposed to the college that they would share the teaching position and do it part-time.

We just now are seeing the first generation of academically trained practitioners proceed through their careers, and with luck, some of them will soon
choose to teach. All of us who have gone before may well have had some academic
training, but it will not have been in public relations. The implications for what
gets taught and how are enormous.

What should be taught in a PR program?

There is a body of knowledge that belongs to public relations. If it can be learned,
it can be taught. By virtue of how the professional practice of public relations
arose historically (as opposed to the history of our tools and techniques), much of
our body of knowledge has come from direct experience. It has been confirmed,
elaborated upon, explained, and enriched by the pieces we have borrowed from
academic disciplines such as psychology and sociology, marketing and business.
The fact that our body of knowledge includes contributions from others is its
strength, because this signature quality is actually a genuine reflection of the nature
of public relations practice itself. The slow march towards formalizing education
in public relations has been characterized by persistent heel-dragging: on the one
hand, by practitioners whose own practices are grounded solely in experience and
who view academics with a measure of contempt; and on the other, academics
who teach in public relations programs but have never practiced, never will, view
knowledge gained experientially with contempt, and likewise, view the practicing
community whom they claim to serve with calculated indifference.

If people from either of these camps had ultimately had their way—or are
allowed to have their way, for they still exist—public relations education would
be very different. As it stands, the courses and programs available in Calgary all
recognize the value of both experiential and theoretical knowledge, and our practice
is the better for it. And yet interestingly, the courses and programs themselves are
all very different.

The courses and programs in question include the full-time now-
Communications degree program at Mount Royal College, the non-credit certificate
program also offered at Mount Royal, the public relations courses offered at SAIT
in its Journalism program, the undergraduate degree in Communications and the
graduate degree in Communications Studies at the University of Calgary, and the
non-credit Management Certificate program in public relations also offered at the
university. What is important to this discussion is that all of the programs have been
strongly influenced by several factors, some of which have been at cross-purposes
from time to time. Those factors include the politics of each of the institutions; the

motivations of the instructional faculty; the vision of the individuals who served on the advisory committees for the programs at each institution (some but not all of whom were practitioners); the priorities of the Calgary chapters of CPRS and IABC; and from time to time, even the interests of the students of these programs.

The "factors" I have just listed are, of course, translated into the actions of individual people, and so the professional perspectives, personalities and agendas of all of these players are what have most strongly influenced the development of the educational programs. Not the least of these were my own views while tenured at Mount Royal College, and later while instructing at the University of Calgary. They are probably the reason for my having been asked to write this chapter!

I have described how the program at Mount Royal College came into being, and more needs to be said about its development. However, at this juncture it is important to describe the evolution of the others.

Courses in the SAIT journalism program

The details as to when public relations courses were introduced to the SAIT journalism program are apparently lost to history, but it is certain that if Mount Royal College's program was not the first to offer public relations education, then

SAIT certainly was. It is also not known whether the impetus for introducing public relations courses into the SAIT program came from industry or from CPRS Calgary (having predated IABC as a presence in Calgary by nearly 20 years), or some other source. In any event, SAIT has offered a few courses in public relations in its journalism program for some 25 years at least.

It would not be surprising if it were longer. If a person were to research all of the public relations programs in North America in particular (because the oldest programs and courses in public relations tend to be located here), the results would show that public relations programs are variously attached to, or embedded within schools of journalism, social sciences, marketing, or business. There are a few oddballs: here and there, public relations may be taught within a psychology department or a creative writing program, for example. Sometimes (though rarely), as is the case with Mount Saint Vincent University's public relations degree program, it even stands alone.

Where a public relations program is located is telling: it often reveals the age of the program, or it reveals the prevailing definition of public relations at the institution itself, or of the faculty members, or the local professional community. Its location absolutely shapes the focus of the curriculum. Since the origins of public relations in North America are historically seen as a media relations response to the journalistic phenomenon of the Muckraking Era of the 1920s, the oldest public relations programs are typically associated with journalism, located in faculties of communication or journalism, and focus on writing as opposed to strategic management of communications. If those proposing a public relations program have come to understand public relations as a marketing or promotional function, it will probably be associated with marketing programs, sometimes within a business faculty, and usually with a marketing support or advertising focus. On the other hand, if public relations is seen primarily as a promotional function, it will probably not be entertained as a serious course of studies at any post-secondary institution.

In this context, it is possible that the courses in the SAIT journalism program predated the program at Mount Royal College, in which case the CPRS-sponsored proposal for the program at the college was based on the view (and this I understand to be true) that public relations practice encompassed more than media relations, and the professional community wished to support a more fulsome program that would train graduates for employment in the field. Nevertheless, over the years, SAIT has never sustained an expansion of its course offerings, although there were years when the public relations-related courses numbered more than two. Individual faculty members had a strong desire to develop a stronger public relations stream, but ultimately it did not develop.

Graduate and undergraduate programs: the University of Calgary

The study of communications came relatively late to the University of Calgary. The Mount Royal College program was well enough established, despite the blow to its credibility in the 1970s. But there were other issues. Because the focus of the college's program was to graduate entry-level prospects to the industry, senior-level practitioners looking for intellectual and professional challenge were left unserved. As well, the growing understanding in the field that the appropriate place for public relations counsel was at the management table fostered the view that public relations education needed to be offered at the graduate level, and not the undergraduate level. The thinking was that undergraduate training produced graduates suitable for entry-level roles, and that public relations practitioners would never move from the level of the tactician to the more strategic and higher level of the counsellor without a higher level of education.

Some combination of these perspectives motivated individual members of the Calgary public relations community as well as CPRS Calgary to approach the University of Calgary with a proposal for a graduate-level degree that would serve senior communicators in Calgary. They partly got their wish. The Master of Communications Studies degree was established in 1983, and Glenna Cross, ABC, was the program's first graduate just a year later in 1984. The curriculum was not narrowly a "public relations" curriculum, but one that responded to the graduate-level needs of a broader population of individuals working in communication-related areas—or who wished to work in communications. Yet the program has always been flexible enough that students could tailor their choice of courses and their work

within those courses to provide the professional development experience they were looking for.

Within a few short years, the undergraduate program was instituted, at least partly to create the full foundational academic stream that would permit the U of C to offer a doctoral degree. At the time, provincial regulations did not allow for the graduate and post-graduate degrees to be in place without the preparatory undergraduate degree as well.

I have always been critical of the undergraduate degree program, which came into being as an afterthought, and without (in my view) due consideration for how it would serve the community. From the outset, the university's calendar described the program as serving students who wished to go into public relations, journalism, broadcasting, the arts, business—the list seemed endless. And yet it always seemed to me that this description was an affront to all of these fields on the basis that each had its own discrete body of knowledge, and each deserved due respect. An appropriate preparation for one was quite different than what would be appropriate for the others—the very argument we in public relations were making to justify not being part of journalism or marketing or creative writing programs.

Non-credit programs: Mount Royal College and the University of Calgary
Despite both the college's and the university's best intentions of serving the public relations community with a range of quality educational opportunities, the fact remained that both institutions' credit programs required students to attend full-time or essentially so, and move in lock-step through the courses. For many working professionals, or for people interested in exploring public relations as a career, the credit programs required more commitment than they were able or willing to give. As a result, Mount Royal College initiated a series of five courses intended to provide volunteers who found themselves doing public relations for non-profit organizations with some grounding in our work. They received a certificate if they completed all five courses. Regrettably many of those who took the courses had higher ambitions: they took the courses and then, with a straight face, told employers they had "taken the course at Mount Royal", implying completion of the much more rigorous diploma program. Employers seldom questioned them.

The need to serve working practitioners with a part-time evening alternative remained, however. Several years after I left Mount Royal College in 1995, I helped the University of Calgary pilot an introductory course in public relations, and after a few semesters and requests from students, the Calgary chapter of IABC, with some participation from CPRS, worked closely with the university to develop a Management Certificate in public relations. Although not a "training program" per se, the courses nevertheless are taught by senior accredited members of one of the two chapters. The program has struggled to find its feet, but not for lack of support by the university. Instead, it is really the lack of response on the part of practitioners themselves to avail themselves of this professional development opportunity, for it remains true that most people holding public relations positions at all levels, but especially the more senior levels, do not have a formal grounding in the body of knowledge of their field.

Mount Royal College's public relations program

The years I spent at Mount Royal College were both the hardest of my life and the most rewarding of my career. Nothing I had done before or have done since has come close to giving me satisfaction the way teaching did. There is nothing that compares with seeing people recognize their own potential, and then realize it by using and building upon tools you have given them.

Given what I have said about the context in which the program existed when I joined the college, my perspective was that the program was well positioned within the institution in a business faculty on equal footing with, but separate from, a journalism program. It had a good practical foundation that, with the injection of some academic elements, had the potential to compete with a degree program such as Mount Saint Vincent's Bachelor of Public Relations. After all, if you were to strip the electives out of most communications degrees, what you would be left with would be the equivalent of the then two-year diploma. Given the program's credibility issues both within and outside the college, the fact was that no one was particularly paying attention as I went about the process of making refinements. In this respect, being the sole instructor in the program gave me the advantage of being able to treat the seven core courses as one entity with seven parts. It took

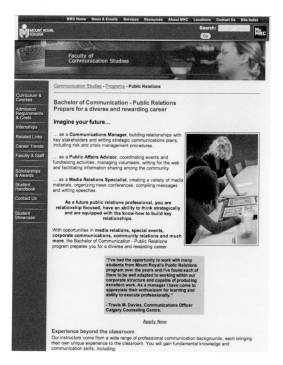

about three years to get it right. I received some measure of external validation for what I had done when the program became just the second ever to have been officially recognized by the Canadian Public Relations Society.

In addition to redeveloping the curriculum, I also had the advantage that the public relations program had just 30 seats, and so in addition to gaining admission to the college through its entrance criteria, which included a basic English skills assessment, prospective students also had to apply to the program itself. They were required to provide three writing samples and write a current events test. They also had to attend a personal interview with me. The college's English skills tests produced results on a six-point scale where a three or four indicated "college-level" skill, and a five or six "university-level" skill. In the first years, it was difficult to find 30 applicants whose results fell into these two categories, and so anyone whose skills were not at the college level at a minimum slipped away quickly. Again, in those early years anyone scoring a five or six automatically got an interview, and unless they did or said something truly egregious, they were admitted to the program—even if they told me their interest in working in public relations was that "they liked people". As the years passed and the number of applicants scoring in the five or six range grew, I tended not to admit those who had no more insight into public relations than that.

The diploma program had included a practicum offering students an opportunity to work with a practitioner for one day a week over 10 weeks. Depending on the type of organization sponsoring the placement, and on the capacity of the practitioner to find something meaningful for a student to do for a day, some of the practicum placements were valuable, some even leading to paid employment for graduates. Other placements were less so, and the value of the practicum was questioned both within the college and in the community. In the mid-1980s, the college entertained the prospect of introducing the relatively new concept of co-operative education to some of its industry-based diploma programs, and I jumped at this opportunity to replace the practicum placements with a much more meaningful workplace experience.

Students integrated two four-month work terms into their academic program, and significantly, they were paid for their work. The idea that students would be paid received some push-back from industry. A number of the employers who had faithfully taken practicum students no longer supported the program. Others, though sceptical at first, quickly revised their opinion when they realized the genuine value the students brought to the workplace, and that the reality was that the students were truly professional and deserved to be paid as such. That having been said, some students were paid poorly, and others very well. Sometimes, it was simply that the placement was an unbudgeted expense, but tantalizing work lay ahead for a student who could afford to take it. Other times, employers in the voluntary sector had only small grants available to them to pay staff, but again, the project work was good. And yes, there were cases where student work was simply undervalued.

The impact of the introduction of co-op education on the program was profound, however. Almost simultaneously, as employers realized the true capability of the students from Mount Royal, the program's reputation grew exponentially.

Applications to the program rose dramatically: in 1988, a record 297 applications were received for the 30 seats in the first-year program. Many of the applications came from newly-graduated (or about-to-be-graduated) university students who were unable to compete with the college's graduates because the university curriculum included no practical skill-based courses specifically in public relations. They brought better writing skills to the program at entry, and often significant work experience as well, so that the college's students were far more accomplished and experienced in the world of work than had previously been the case. They also made it possible to introduce more challenge into the curriculum, and so these graduates became hot properties on the employment market. Several were actually hired by their co-op education employers and given leave to return to the college to complete their diplomas.

Over the next five or six years, the program's reputation was firmly established on the strength of the graduates whose performance continued to impress employers, and whose employability record also kept the application rate at, or near the top of the list of programs most in demand at the college. This performance record is also what positioned the public relations program for readiness when the Province of Alberta indicated cautious willingness to consider degree-granting status for colleges. The context was that the province was under extreme pressure to expand the capacity at Alberta's post-secondary institutions, and Mount Royal College was at the forefront of the lobbying effort, having provided university transfer courses for many years. If the college could offer university-quality instruction at far less cost than the universities, why could it not offer degrees?

If you consider what I have said earlier about the historical developments in the practice of public relations—the gravitation away from our journalistic roots, the aspirations towards professionalization, the emergence of a distinctive body of knowledge—you may perhaps appreciate why I remain convinced that for the public relations program to truly respond to the needs of the industry and its practitioners, it needed to stand alone as a Bachelor of Public Relations degree, and as such, serve as a Western counterpart to the Mount Saint Vincent program in Halifax. It also deserved to stand alone, having become one of the strongest and most successful programs the college then had to offer. However, the same forces that I identified earlier as being critically influential in the establishment of our public relations education programs were also brought to bear on the decision relating to degree-granting status. As other colleges in the province scrambled to pull together proposals so that they could mount pilot projects, the clear signal from government was that the number of pilots would be very few, and that no single

Education is the cornerstone of a profession, and CPRS Calgary has enthusiastically supported the development of PR courses and programs for most of its 50 years.

institution would get more than two or three. This announcement intensified the political jockeying that had taken over life at the college. The initial nine contenders were winnowed down to three or four, one of which was a proposal for a Bachelor of Applied Communications under which there would be three streams: technical writing (from the Faculty of Arts), journalism, and public relations. This proposal was ultimately accepted by the province as one of the pilots approved for Mount Royal College, and implemented by the college.

I did not participate in this work. My view was that by locating public relations with journalism and writing programs, the optics alone took our field back 50 years. I had spent too many years trying to carry the program forward, and had staked my own reputation on doing so. I chose this moment to leave the college.

And so it goes

In some ways, the Calgary market remains unique if not remarkable for the fact that we have three post-secondary institutions all offering programs intended to serve employers wanting to hire communicators. Do they serve those needs well? Do they serve our industry well? Those questions, gentle reader, I leave to you to answer. But I would conclude with this observation: in recent years, both CPRS Calgary and IABC Calgary have seen stable if not steadily increasing levels of membership. The number of accredited practitioners in Calgary is higher than in many other markets, especially on a percentage basis. Our practitioners are increasingly taking top honours in professional awards programs. I'm convinced that the presence of educational opportunities here is partly behind these trends. I'm convinced education truly is the cornerstone of a profession and that public relations has every potential for reaching that goal. But it will take the collective will and the vision of practitioners to make it so.

Elaine Dixson, APR, ABC, is President of Key Concepts Ltd. She taught the public relations program at Mount Royal College from 1984 to 1995, during which time the program evolved from a two-year diploma program to degree-readiness, and one of the college's first co-operative education programs. Prior to joining Mount Royal College, she worked in several public and private organizations, and now consults to a range of organizations in public, private, and non-profit sectors. She holds a Bachelor's degree in Journalism, a Master's degree in Communications Studies, and a Master's degree in Continuing Education. She is accredited by the Canadian Public Relations Society (and holds membership in the Public Relations Society of America) and by the International Association of Business Communicators. She was honoured with IABC's Master Communicator Award in 2004. She served as Chief Examiner (English) with the CPRS Accreditation Council from 1995 to 2000.

Monique Chenier: "Home-based consulting allowed me to schedule my work when I was most creative."

9

Working from Home:

Then and now

By Monique Chenier

For decades, PR consulting in Calgary meant agencies. But in recent years there has been significant growth in the number of individuals who are consulting from home. This chapter takes a look at why this growth has occurred, and examines it from a "then" and "now" perspective.

Back in the 1950s, when CPRS Calgary was just getting started, "PR men" from industry and government would meet for lunch to share their public relations experiences over 35-cent drinks at the Palliser Hotel. But what about consultants? In fact, some of the society's earliest documents, on yellowing paper at Calgary's Glenbow Archives, reveal that there was one public relations consultant working from a home-based office, and he was an active participant in the society almost from the beginning.

THEN: Consulting in Calgary in the 1960s

In the inaugural bylaws, dated 1958, independent consultants were a recognized category for membership in CPRS. The bylaws identified "persons who spend a major part of their time as public relations counsellors in independent practice," as well as salaried staff of an established organization and instructors in a course on public relations.

Although the first few years of elected CPRS Calgary executives hailed mainly from corporations and government, the 1959/60 membership roster lists one lone consultant among the 26 Alberta members: John D. Francis. John was soon elected to the CPRS Calgary Board of Directors, sending out the 1961 notice for the society's annual meeting and elections.

After working in the corporate sector for a number of years, John Francis, APR, FCPRS(H), began consulting in 1958 and for the first couple of years was working from home. He and his wife Lois and daughter Susan lived in Spruce Cliff apartments. "For a while I rode the bus downtown to visit clients, bringing my notes home and typing them, including carbon copies, on a portable," says John. "Riding the bus wasn't a total waste—I got chatting with a *Herald* reporter,

Merv Anderson, who took an interest in what I was doing. A few years later Merv became City Editor. It was helpful to have a personal contact of this nature."

As is still the case today, networking was critical to building a solid client base in the early years. "One of my ways of networking was I joined the Junior Chamber of Commerce," explains John. "The Jaycees were very active at the time—every member was expected to work on a committee. I met lots of young guys who were trying to get ahead. Some became clients, and many became life-long friends."

NOW: Consulting in Calgary in the new millennium

As a 10-year public relations "veteran," I hadn't considered consulting in my career path. Although I guess I shouldn't have been surprised, since PR hadn't been on my radar either. I moved to Calgary from Winnipeg with a Bachelor's degree in Interior Design from the University of Manitoba. After an unsatisfying stint at a small architectural firm, a door opened to a communications position in a growing company.

After working in corporate communications for nearly 10 years, I was down-sized from an oilfield equipment manufacturer in the industry downturn after 9/11. It seemed like the perfect opportunity to change direction—I sent out a letter to my network re-introducing myself as a consultant.

Advances in technology from the days of the typewriter made it quick, easy and inexpensive to set up a home office. Working from home was a refreshing change from a corporate culture that expected everyone to be in the office by 7 a.m. Home-based consulting allowed me to schedule my work when I was most creative and, for me, that often meant evenings. It also meant I could be home to take care of my 15-year-old dog—I'm pretty sure Luci lived many years longer with me at home than she would have spending long and lonely days on her own.

THEN: Staying connected in the 1970s and 1980s

One of the challenges of home-based consulting is staying connected—benefit-ing from the synergy that comes from interacting and brainstorming with co-workers. Merriam-Webster's dictionary defines networking as "the exchange of information or services among individuals, groups or institutions." But for con-sultants, networking is so much more—it is one of the critical cornerstones of a successful career.

As a consultant for most of his career, long-time CPRS Calgary member Don Boynton, APR, remembers one way consultants stayed connected. "I think that it is notable that during the 1970s and 1980s there was a national CPRS Consultants' Institute. Members were affiliated with the PRSA Counselors Academy and we had a semi-active Calgary Consultants' Section that, like Calgary's current Indy500 group, distinguished professional consultants from less-than-professional people offering public relations services.

"In the 1980s, we cooperated in a CPRS consultants display ad in the Yellow Pages," recalls Don. "The ad was credited with generating new business for several of us, too!"

The Consultants' Section was just gaining steam when a session entitled *Professionalism and Business: Working Together Through CPRS* was presented at the 1977 CPRS National Conference in Halifax, Nova Scotia. The speaker was Peter G. Osgood, a member of the Public Relations Society of America Counselors Academy.

Peter spoke about how he had benefitted from his membership in the Counselors Academy. "I get new ideas. We tend to share information about new services and methods more than one might suspect." He went on to explain that "another competitor has shown us how they are profitably using a computer—for more than just financial information and management reports. This, too, opens new avenues of thinking."

NOW: Staying connected in the 2000s

Keeping in touch has never been easier than in this era of instant communications via the Internet, with email, text-messaging and social media like YouTube and Facebook. However, networking face-to-face with like-minded team members and others is invaluable to testing ideas and problem solving. What's a home-based consultant to do?

Starting as an independent consultant in 2002, I found the element I most missed about corporate work was the direct contact with my co-workers. Although I did have regular interaction with my clients, I missed the synergy that comes from spontaneous brainstorming among team members.

In late 2003, I put forward to the CPRS Calgary Board the idea of a networking group of home-based consultants. The goal of the Indy500 initiative was to help CPRS Calgary's independents accelerate their businesses through marketing opportunities, online consultant directory and resources, business management support, networking and problem-solving support.

The initial gathering of the Indy500 in early 2005, appropriately located at a local independent coffee house, attracted seven CPRS consultants. We all agreed that there was value in meeting to build relationships with fellow consultants, learn each other's strengths, and discover what kind of work individuals prefer and would like more of for referral purposes.

An email from long-time consultant and Indy500 participant Judi Gunter, APR, validated our approach: "I think for me the Indy500 is going to be a very neat solution to the need to get a higher value from CPRS than I am getting now, stay connected with like-minded independent practitioners, have access to occasional opportunities, and experience a group as catalyst to get out there and hustle in order to ensure there is always a little something billable on the go for me at all times."

The group continues to meet several times a year to share ideas or learn from guest speakers. Recent events have included a discussion with an intellectual property lawyer and an IT specialist discussing technology options for home-based businesses. Rarely a week goes by when the spirit of cooperation isn't thriving among the group—consulting opportunities are regularly emailed among members of the Indy500.

THEN: Evolution of public relations consulting

Those who have never known a workplace without computers will have difficulty imagining how one worked from home without all the technological conveniences we take for granted today. Maureen Payne, likely one of the first women in Calgary to start a home-based consulting business, has been working primarily from home since 1981.

She recalls early on a "$1,000 writing contract for the Queen's visit while juggling two small kids, an elderly father, and planting her petunias." In the early 1980s, the tools of the trade included a typewriter, the "most antiquated phone" and driving to deliver scripts to her client for review. And while the personal situation of children, parents and other commitments is the reason many consultants choose to work from home, technology has certainly made the job much more efficient.

In addition to technology, another element of consulting that has changed is the scope of work offered by consultants. Judi Gunter, who has been consulting from a home office since 1995, has seen the big and small cycles. "For a while," she says, "it was all about big, integrated advertising/PR/marketing 'jack of all trades' agencies because clients wanted that 'one-stop shop'.

"Then it gave way to the independents and small boutique firms that focused on PR, which then hooked up with advertising, marketing or research agencies or other specialists as needed." In Judi's experience, "Clients wanted the personal service. They wanted to know that the person to whom they gave the business was the person doing the work."

While a great deal has changed, much has remained the same. The reasons clients choose to work with independent consultants are as relevant today as they were 50 years ago. CPRS Calgary records include a copy of an undated booklet produced by the CPRS Toronto Consultants' Section, entitled *Public Relations Consulting—What's It All About?* One of the sections—*Why use consultants?*—answered the question this way: "There is no long-range commitment by the client company, no new employee overhead and benefits responsibilities, and the services of highly skilled public relations people become immediately available to deal with the organization's communication problem."

NOW: The future

The independent consultant has never been in greater demand. From filling term positions or taking on one-time projects, to serving as the communications strategist and tactician for small organizations or supplementing the communications teams of large corporations, home-based consultants today are enjoying challenging work in a robust economy.

In 1959/60, CPRS Calgary reported having one consultant out of 26 members. In a December 1992, CPRS Calgary membership survey, 8 per cent of respondents were listed as consultants. Now, in 2008, CPRS Calgary has more than 20 per cent of members categorized as consultants. (These last two statistics don't differentiate between independents and agency consultants. However, clearly much of the growth has been in home-based consultants.)

The steady growth in numbers demonstrates that consulting—agency and home-based—is on the rise as a legitimate career aspiration for those public relations professionals with the experience and education—not to mention a dynamic network of contacts—to offer strategic PR counsel to their clients. It will be fascinating to see how public relations in general, and consulting in particular, continue to evolve. But it's a good bet that home-based PR consultants will continue to expand their influence, and continue their 50-year tradition of active participation in CPRS Calgary.

Monique Chenier spent 10 years in corporate communications, and has been a sole proprietor in public relations consulting for the past six years. A member of CPRS since 1998, Monique has held several CPRS Calgary Board positions, most recently serving as Chair of the successful 2005 CPRS National Conference. She also sits as Presiding Officer of a newly-formed national committee providing guidance and leadership for the annual CPRS conference. As the next logical step in her thriving consulting career, Monique recently fused with two other consultants to open their own agency.

DESCRIPTION *SIGNALEMENT*

	Bearer *Titulaire*	Wife *Femme*
Profession / *Profession*	Student	
Place and date of birth / *Lieu et date de naissance*	Dartford England 1 Oct. 1943	
Country of Residence / *Pays de Résidence*	Canada	
Height / *Taille*	5 ft. 7 in.	ft. in.
Colour of eyes / *Couleur des yeux*	Blue	
Colour of hair / *Couleur des cheveux*		
Special peculiarities / *Signes particuliers*		

CHILDREN *ENFANTS*

Name *Nom*   Date of birth *Date de naissance*   Sex *Sexe*

CANCELLED

Usual signature of bearer
Signature du titulaire

Peter McKenzie Brown

Bearer
Titulaire

Wife
Femme

(PHOTO)

Peter McKenzie-Brown's 1970 passport photo:
Peter took a most unusual route into PR, starting
out as a teacher of Transcendental Meditation,
and then going to work for Gulf and Big Oil.

10 Breaking into Public Relations:

How CPRS Calgary members got their start

By Jodi Currie

In the early days of CPRS Calgary, the majority of members started as journalists. Today, PR professionals are likely to have a degree in public relations or communications, perhaps a Master's degree, or perhaps multiple degrees. And then there are individuals who took altogether different routes into PR and still succeeded. Here's how a few CPRS members made their way into the business.

In the late 1950s, when CPRS Calgary first found its roots in Calgary, there were no communications degree programs in Canada. Many of the practitioners at that time, and still many today, came to public relations through other avenues, usually from radio or newspapers. Still, some came through rather obscure and unlikely channels.

Peter McKenzie-Brown (CPRS Calgary member from 1977 to 1983) earned a Bachelor's degree in Philosophy from MacMurray College in the United States. After migrating to Canada as an anti-war protestor and having a close encounter with Maharishi Mahesh Yogi, he began teaching Transcendental Meditation in Toronto. He enjoyed the teaching but not the associated paycheque, and after almost six years began looking for a change.

Peter moved to Calgary, staying in the house of a friend named Vernon Barnes. Before he even began looking for a job, the phone rang. It was a recruiter from Gulf Canada calling to talk to Vernon. After a brief chat, Peter happily agreed to apply for a job in public relations, working for Brock Hammond. That was the beginning of a life-long career.

While Peter's story is unconventional, the majority of the early members of CPRS Calgary did come from the traditional journalism background. Jim Rennie, Sr. worked as a reporter for *The Edmonton Journal* and *The Edmonton Bulletin* (no longer in existence) prior to the Second World War. After a tour of duty as a navigator in a Lancaster bomber, Jim stayed on to work as a war correspondent for Southam in Europe. After the war, he returned to Edmonton ready to pick up his newspaper career just as Imperial Oil struck black gold in Leduc. They began to hire newspaper people to act as public relations representatives and Jim began his new career in PR.

He worked in Edmonton, Toronto and Vancouver, and then was transferred to Calgary in 1954 where he stayed until his retirement in 1973. Jim was one of the founding members of CPRS Calgary and his son, also Jim Rennie, continued his legacy years later.

John Francis, founder of Francis, William & Johnson Ltd. (FWJ) and an early member of CPRS Calgary, got his start in public relations from his days as an ad salesman and eventual director of the University of Alberta yearbook—the *Evergreen and Gold*. John took his Bachelor of Commerce degree at the U of A and advertising sales commissions helped defray his costs. In 1950, university fees were $165 per term and housing was $60 a month.

Jim Rennie, Sr. was one of the founding members of the society. As was the norm back then, his background was the news media, having been a reporter for *The Edmonton Journal* and *The Edmonton Bulletin.*

After returning to Calgary from an eight-month European hitchhiking adventure, John was surprised to see his experience publishing the yearbook had just as much impact on his future potential employers as his degree. He was soon hired as the assistant to the Director of Public Relations with Calgary Power (now TransAlta), with his main assignment being editor of the company's house organ, the *Relay*.

John had been thinking about earning a law degree, however he liked the work he was doing and the positive characteristics of public relations. He also realized he could get his Master's within one or two years, and with a family it was important to get busy earning a living as soon as possible.

At that time there were two universities offering Master's programs in public relations—one was Boston University and the other was New York University. With the help of family and friends, John packed up his wife and new daughter Susan and moved to Boston in September 1956. There were just 25 students in the B.U. program. They came from across the U.S. and had diverse backgrounds, which enriched the educational experience.

After one year of study, John was able to move back to Calgary to complete his thesis—*Public Relations Problems of American Petroleum Companies in Canada*. He researched his thesis by interviewing oil company executives and newspaper editors—great contacts for his future work.

In the end, thesis and degree—a Master of Science degree in Public Relations—in hand, nobody offered John a job. The year 1957 was a real downer for the petroleum industry and public relations was looked on as a marginally beneficial service. "In fact I'm 76 and still waiting to be offered a job," says John. So he started out on his own as an independent PR practitioner. Thus began a firm that became one of Alberta's largest and most respected advertising and public relations agencies—FWJ.

John has been a member of CPRS Calgary since 1959. He attained his APR in the first year it was offered. He won many CPRS awards including the CPRS Lamp of Service, CPRS Award of Attainment, Honourary Fellow and Life Membership, and has won numerous awards in CPRS creative competitions. He served as Calgary President, and National President of the society.

John Francis, the dean of Calgary consultants, was one of the first CPRS Calgary members with PR-related academic credentials. He obtained a Master of Science degree in Public Relations from Boston University in 1958.

Cynthia Balfour (CPRS Calgary member from 1972 to 1984) began her career in public relations by a long series of fortuitous events. Even as a child in New Zealand she wanted to be a writer and complete the great New Zealand novel, but life and happenstance would intervene and put Cynthia's plans on hold for 26 years.

Going to university for journalism during the war years was not an option so her dreams took a back seat as she settled for nursing training. However, Cupid stepped in and before Cynthia finished her training she was married to a young air force officer and soon found herself a "farmer's wife".

In the early 1960s, Cynthia was living in England and started a job with an advertising agency in London doing market research—a new tool in advertising at the time. In 1964, and back in New Zealand, her first job was with one of New Zealand's largest building companies, followed by a position in a large advertising agency. Next was a writing job for a ski magazine then an editorial assistant for a weekly financial publication. Unfortunately this last position only lasted six months before the publication folded.

By now though, Cynthia was getting interested in more aspects of the publishing business and turned her attention to printing. She got a job in a very small publishing business and spent the first couple of days in the print shop learning all she could. However, her position was as a sales rep and Cynthia only lasted two weeks—but she had learned a great deal about the business and soon she was hired by a small publishing house. Now she was beginning to achieve some real success, just in time for a move to Calgary in 1967.

She got a job with a small advertising agency mainly writing copy for radio and going to client meetings. But the highlight was being involved in the Husky Tower (now the Calgary Tower), which was under construction. Cynthia would coordinate photographers for publicity shots which entailed riding in the construction elevator on the outside of the tower and then literally walking the plank to reach the platform.

After about 18 months, Cynthia had become acclimatized to the Calgary media scene and was ready to move on. She applied for a job with FWJ but had been warned that John Francis would never hire someone without some kind of tertiary degree. She proved them wrong and is happy to say, in her experience, learning on the job had just as many advantages as a degree.

Cynthia Balfour took a circuitous route to a career in public relations, working first as a writer and in advertising in New Zealand before moving to Calgary in 1967.

Henry Stevens, Vice-President at NATIONAL Public Relations in Calgary, really wanted to be an on-air radio host. He worked at his school radio station and after graduation he attended the B.C. Institute of Technology for its broadcast communications program.

After completing the diploma in the early 1980s, Henry fulfilled his dream, becoming the evening/overnight DJ at a radio station in Castlegar, B.C. He soon realized the newsroom was a better "gig"—better hours to start with. He made a switch to the news side and loved it. He soon worked in newsrooms in Kelowna and Victoria.

In 1987, after returning from extensive overseas traveling, Henry moved his family to Calgary. He worked in radio for a while but was looking at other ways his journalism experience could work for him. Why not PR?

Henry applied for, and was accepted into, the public relations diploma program at Mount Royal College and hasn't looked back since.

In the 1970s, a handbook was typed up as a primer for those interested in the public relations field. One chapter, titled *Breaking into Public Relations*, states, "While there is probably no clear-cut formula for getting a job in most lines of work, this seems especially true for public relations. To date, the pattern generally persists whereby entry is made after some experience has been obtained in another occupation, usually some segment of journalism."

Many years later and with a variety of public relations undergraduate degree and Master's programs to educate those interested in a career in PR, we still find many are coming via alternate routes.

When Monique Chenier (CPRS Calgary member since 1998) earned a Bachelor's degree in Interior Design in 1989 she never thought it would lead to public relations. Her first job with an architectural firm was a junior role including some administrative work like typing proposals. When the Office Manager resigned, Monique was given her role—as the only other woman in the office—which meant no hands-on design work, so she left.

Henry Stevens, Vice-President at NATIONAL Public Relations, started out in broadcasting, as a DJ.

While looking for other work, Monique took various temporary jobs, mostly administrative work, but her last position was with a small company launching a new division. She worked with their business development group to set up the launch event. They were so impressed with her strong writing and organizational skills they offered her a full-time job. To add to her skills she completed the Marketing Management certificate at the University of Calgary and advanced through six positions in seven years culminating in her role as Communications Services Manager.

Monique says many people have commented how she "wasted" her degree but she believes many of the basic skills she learned in interior design are transferable to public relations. "An interior designer researches the users and uses for the space—how they work and live within that space. She analyzes data to determine the most effective, efficient and aesthetically pleasing way to meet their needs. She designs the space and works with various contractors to ensure it is built to her detailed specifications. And, she evaluates the results so that all the user requirements have been met—all within strict timelines and budgets. It's really not that much different than what we do with the RACE formula, is it?"

A special report celebrating the 60th Anniversary of the Master of Science degree in public relations at Boston University shows they are experiencing an increasing diversity in the educational backgrounds of students applying to the program. "Graduate students who have studied English or journalism are still most common, but sociology, psychology and even engineering students are joining." [1]

Brent Shervey, Managing Director of Boyden, an executive search firm in Calgary, says there are way more people who consider themselves communications professionals now than there used to be. There are people with certificates, degrees (Bachelor's and Master's) and accreditations who all claim to be communications professionals, and the market can get confused.

With public relations gaining more credibility and understanding over the past 50 years, employers are able to focus exactly what their needs are to find the candidate(s) who meet their specific requirements. Each company (client) is different but proven experience is still an important asset—ideally experience in a similar company in the same or related field (especially for intermediate and senior level positions). Also, Brent says proven leadership experience supervising, coaching and mentoring staff and an understanding of the business are extremely important. He believes a good communications person should know more about the client's business than the client does. Of course, bringing a diversity of talent, experience and education to the table can help you outshine your competition.

There is such a plethora of programs in Calgary now, at the University of Calgary, Mount Royal College and the Southern Alberta Institute of Technology—not to mention the online programs through universities and colleges across North America and the U.K. Many of the graduates in Calgary want to stay in the city and all come into the market around the same time. Brent says it's no wonder it's tough for many of them to find that first professional job.

Jamie Popadiuk (CPRS Calgary student member since 2008) completed the SAIT journalism program and decided to pursue her communications degree through Royal Roads' online learning. She felt earning a degree was important but she also hopes a combination of the complementary programs and her degree will help her find a position she's attracted to and earn a higher salary in her career.

One interesting observation of young people joining the workforce is they are finding the reality of public relations positions is not what they learned in school. While the requirements for entrance at the basic level are pretty well defined, public relations means different things to different organizations (for example, media relations, marketing communications, events, and even social media). And with the amount of specialization now compared to the past—government relations, investor relations, community investment and more—it is not possible, nor desirable, to offer a broad-based definition of public relations which can be "dumbed down" for everyone.

Practitioners have worked hard to establish ethical guidelines, develop standards of practice and earn the reputation that public relations enjoys today. When a group of Calgary practitioners got together to begin a Calgary chapter of CPRS in the 1950s, the practice of public relations was not well known and was largely misunderstood. Many people then, and even in more recent years, "stumbled" into the business, but public relations has experienced tremendous growth and organizations have seen the value effective communications can have on their business. Public relations no longer has to justify itself to management as it did in its early years, and in many corporations today the senior PR officer is on the management or operating committee. Young professionals are now making the conscious decision to practice public relations and are working to earn the communications degrees they will need to hopefully land that first job. However, you will still be able to find those who came to the profession through alternative, and often seemingly unrelated fields, who have and will achieve great success in their careers.

Jodi Currie received a diploma in Broadcasting from Mount Royal College in 1999. After a number of years as a radio copywriter, and shooter and editor in television, she began work with a local, small marketing communications agency. She earned a certificate in basic public relations through the Mount Royal College continuing education program. Jodi has been a member of CPRS Calgary since 2005. She has been a part of the CPRS Calgary website committee since 2005 and has served on the CPRS Calgary Board since 2007. She is the Manager, Communications for The Kidney Foundation of Canada Southern Alberta Branch.

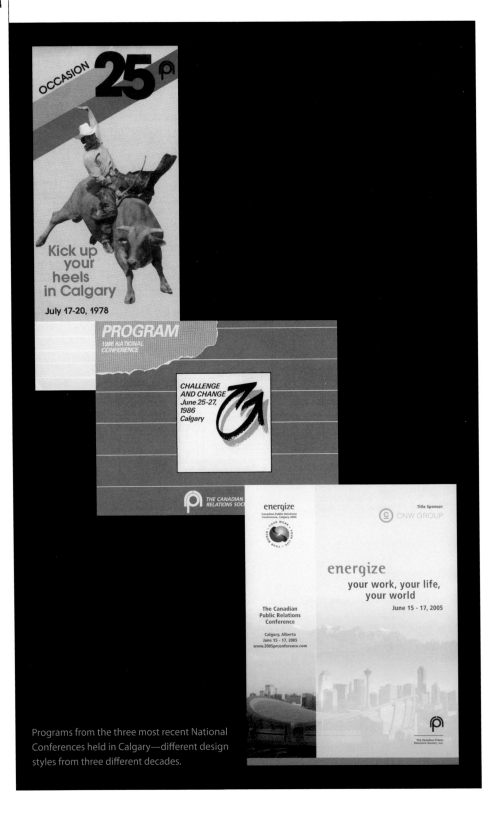

OCCASION 25 ℗

Kick up
your
heels
in Calgary

July 17-20, 1978

PROGRAM
1986 NATIONAL
CONFERENCE

CHALLENGE
AND CHANGE
June 25-27,
1986
Calgary

℗ THE CANADIAN
RELATIONS SOC

energize
Canadian Public Relations
Conference, Calgary 2005

Title Sponsor:
ⓒ CNW GROUP

energize
your work, your life,
your world
June 15 - 17, 2005

The Canadian
Public Relations
Conference

Calgary, Alberta
June 15 - 17, 2005
www.2005prconference.com

℗
The Canadian Public
Relations Society, Inc.

Programs from the three most recent National
Conferences held in Calgary—different design
styles from three different decades.

11 Chairing a National Conference:

Focused on professional development and value for money spent

By Joe Will, APR

CPRS Calgary organized and has been the host society for four National Conferences. The first conference was in 1968, organized by a committee chaired by John Thorburn. T.A.G. Watson chaired the 1978 conference committee, Joe Will chaired the 1986 conference committee, and Monique Chenier chaired the 2005 conference committee. All four conferences were well organized, and considered to be highly successful in terms of setting new benchmarks for attendance and revenues raised. This is the story of the work that went into organizing one of those conferences, what worked well and what could have been improved.

When Don Boynton, then President of CPRS Calgary, approached me to chair the organizing of the 1986 National Conference, I deferred giving an answer. I wanted to talk to my good friend and colleague, Jim Rennie, about sitting on the Organizing Committee, and I wanted clearance from my employer. When I approached Jim, he, too, had a condition; he wanted responsibility for the conference program and assurance that he'd have control to do it without interference. That was fine with me. My employer had some reluctance about my participation, but also agreed.

Twenty-three years later, when Jim asked me to contribute my reminiscences on the National Conference of 1986, my immediate response was: "Well, of course." A more visceral reaction crept up over the next few days along the lines of "What have I gotten myself into?"

I left the world of full-time public relations three years after that National Conference to pursue my interest and ultimately my "next" career in the wine business. Things like the National Conference have not been exactly top-of-mind and have been overlain by many subsequent events. My several moves of location and the associated purges of possessions have left me zero files or memorabilia from a long-gone era.

But time and events did not bury everything.

The first and most vivid memory was of another friend and colleague, the aforementioned Don Boynton, arriving like a proud father with a grin that only he could muster to deliver the final conference program. His pride was well placed—the program was lovely. That, and his demeanour, softened the resolve of those who would have done him grievous bodily harm. Don was arriving with the programs in a taxi as delegates were entering the conference hotel and registering; there had been some anxiety about their delivery.

Other memories began to emerge, some on their own, and others were triggered by materials that Jim had kept or discovered in his research: notes for a presentation that I prepared about the conference, a final wrap-up report prepared by the Organizing Committee, a list of volunteers, a typed copy of the final program. I've drawn heavily on these materials for this report.

The CPRS National Council met during the 1978 Western-themed National Conference in Calgary—which explains the Western attire on some of the Calgary representatives, including *(from left to right)* Leo Van Vugt, Jim Rennie, Jr., T.A.G. Watson, Cynthia Balfour and David McAsey.

While I was the Conference Chair, I was not the driving force. The collective effort of the Organizing Committee and the individual leadership of its members caused it to happen and to be a success.

The initial work to secure the National Conference for Calgary, to establish the dates of June 25 to 27, and to book conference facilities at the Westin Hotel, was done by others well in advance.

Planning for the conference began in earnest 16 months before the event with the first meeting of the Organizing Committee. The discussion was largely conceptual—we deliberately stayed away from details—as we sought to define what we wanted the conference to accomplish. This led to a mission statement and six major goals for the conference. These contributed to a common perspective for the committee and volunteers.

Two concepts stood out: a commitment to excellent professional development and a commitment to providing delegates with value for their money.

And money stood out in another way—we could not afford to lose any. The Calgary chapter did not have the resources to cover a deficit and the National Society was depending on a surplus from the conference to help fund its programming.

The planning quickly moved from the conceptual stage to define the most important conference jobs and to organize them into four major task areas. This was reflected in the Organizing Committee—it had four Vice-Chairmen, one responsible for each major task area, along with the Chair and two members at large. The structure evolved and expanded by three as new needs were recognized.

One of the successes of the conference was the committees and work teams that developed with 75 people participating, many of them CPRS non-members. They were a cross-section of the public relations community—from corporations, government, academia, consultancies, and the not-for-profit sector. And they ranged from new arrivals to senior executives. These many people and the jobs they did built a solid conference.

And the heart of it was its program. Jim and his Program Committee built the main attraction that would bring in the delegates and deliver a rewarding experience. Its core was professional development supported by exciting, lively social events and an interesting partners program.

In the conference wrap-up report, Jim noted the programs were initially developed as a group, with input from all members; then individuals headed up sub-committees to attend to details for specific areas.

"The basic approach was to develop a top-quality professional development program, with some things of interest to all ranges of public relations practitioners, but with a greater-than-usual emphasis on items for the more-senior person (e.g. issues, management, academic/research). Within the over-all *Challenge and Change* theme, the committee also built on sub-themes of international public relations and 'new technology' in public relations.

"We wanted to attract a variety of speakers, from a variety of backgrounds and disciplines (academic, consulting, government, corporate), and from a variety of regions…We wanted to force delegates to have to choose from an over-abundance of quality speakers, not have too few. We also wanted a variety of formats to maintain interest—panels and discussions involving the audience, seminars and workshops that could involve hands-on demonstrations and case studies that reviewed the basics of public relations in action."

The basic program outline was developed a year before the conference; it was reviewed with National, regional societies and special sections, and their suggestions were incorporated into the planning. The program was confirmed by March 1986 with 34 of the first 35 people contacted accepting the invitation to speak. Only two speakers bowed out, and they were replaced within 48 hours. The conference agreed to cover speaker costs, as necessary, but none received any fee or honorarium.

In fact, many of the speakers—such as well-known U.S. communications academics James Grunig and Norman Nager—were so interested in visiting Calgary (and Banff) that fees and honorariums were never an issue.

The committee was also thorough in all the details—including keeping contact with speakers, setting expectations for sessions, finding moderators, and ensuring the setup for each session. Speaker breakfasts each morning got moderators and panel members together; one moderator failed to show, as discovered at breakfast, and a replacement was quickly found.

The Program Chairman used a CPRS Calgary Town Crier Awards bell to get people moving into sessions. It was hard not to move when the bell clanged. And people wanted in to the sessions—there was a good range of topics from management to issues to techniques. The speakers had good content and their presentations were mostly excellent.

All events occurred on time, all speakers showed up on time, and all audio-visual equipment was set up as per speakers' requests. The professional development program received an overwhelmingly favourable response in the exit survey of delegates. Attendance was considered good at 250 delegates (although we had hoped for more) and the numbers coming to individual sessions were generally consistent.

Also receiving good marks were the partners program and evening social sessions, which followed a Western theme. This theme was not embraced by all and generated lots of discussion. The Program Committee reasoned that Western is what Calgary does well, is emblematic of the city and is what visitors expect. The theme was confirmed—and it worked. The first evening social event was dinner at Heritage Park with entertainment, a ride on the paddlewheeler Moyie, and other attractions at the park; the following night was the President's Ball at the hotel with Western formal dress, a casino, auction and dance. All generated good response and a high level of delegate participation.

Another key component of the conference experience was the work of Yvonne Adam, Vice-Chair of Operations. Yvonne, an independent consultant, and her committee were dedicated to doing a good job. She noted in the wrap-up report: "Delegates ultimately judge the conference by what they experience. Capture them by being on top of details…look for and solve the little problems that can detract from delegate satisfaction."

Her team was responsible for facilities and hotel liaison, including registration, catering, signage, interpretation, audio-visual equipment/systems and transportation. She kept her committee small, with each person taking a specific task area, and they kept current with short, frequent meetings. The hotel contact was limited to two persons and they stayed on top of facility changes as conference preparations proceeded.

The registration function was highly organized and it was open from 7 a.m. until the last daily event was under way. The only glitch was a name-tag system, supplied at no cost by an exhibitor; it did not work as well as expected, causing backlogs and frustration.

Great success was achieved in the catering area through good management and close liaison with the hotel. The hotel needed confirmed numbers for each meal and Yvonne's job was to deal with the uncertainty of how many delegates would want to be fed at any particular meal. We didn't want to waste, with one eye on our budget, and we didn't want to disappoint. The hotel was accommodating, ready with an extra table and chairs as the room was about to overflow, and on one occasion a handful of co-operating delegates modestly enjoyed the hotel dining room at conference expense.

Audio taping of conference sessions and simultaneous French-English translation provided a few challenges. Ultimately, many of the audio tapes were not of sufficient quality to be useful as a replay of a session. And translation services were used consistently by only two or three delegates, and for some sessions were not used at all.

Overall, it was a smooth operation and Yvonne reported in the end that "the entire committee worked well together as a single unit—we liked and respected each other even after it was all over—and we had fun! What more could we ask for?"

The delegates had fun, too. And getting them to Calgary and to the conference fell in large part to Don Boynton who came forward a few months into the planning process when the original Vice-Chair of Communications was unable to continue.

Don and his committee were responsible for developing and executing a plan to market to all potential delegates, including production of materials, mailings, advertising, airline negotiations and media relations.

The most recent National Conference held in Calgary was in 2005. A strong professional development program, featuring speakers such as noted pollster Allan Gregg, drew excellent crowds.

They were quick to come up with the theme for the conference—*Challenge and Change*—and a logo-like visual identity that could be used in print materials and any other promotional materials. Using the conference program as their main selling point, they set out to reach public relations professionals and related disciplines.

They started with an inexpensive flatsheet that was distributed at two Canadian IABC conferences in September 1985 and the PRSA conference two months later. This was followed by a detailed draft program in January, six months before the conference, that was sent to professional media and national news media. An updated draft program, and registration form, was published the next month in the CPRS National newsletter.

Bennett Freeman, Managing Director and International Practice Leader, Corporate Social Responsibility, for Burson-Marsteller in Washington, D.C. also spoke at the 2005 conference. CPRS Calgary co-sponsored his presentation, along with the Communications and Public Relations Foundation, as the first annual Diana and Charles Tisdall Lecture in Communications.

The committee also researched and developed a list of 500 non-members drawing from special interest groups and related professions. This list, along with CPRS (and IABC) members, received a fully designed preliminary program and registration form. It had been professionally produced by a sponsor (Nova, an Alberta Corporation) and mailed at little cost to the conference by Travel Alberta, a department of the provincial government.

Canada NewsWire produced a video news release (at no cost) about the upcoming conference, which was distributed to all CPRS chapters for screening at luncheon meetings.

A sub-committee with volunteers in key market chapters of Edmonton, Vancouver, and Toronto conducted a telephone solicitation of members. A follow-up mailing was made to all CPRS members (at no cost, by the Calgary Stampede) and a reminder flyer went in the last National newsletter before the conference.

The fourth of the original task areas was Sponsorship and its importance reflected our concern about having a financially-successful conference, particularly one that did not incur a deficit.

Don Smith, Manager of Public Affairs at Amoco Canada Petroleum, put together a blue-ribbon committee that included several senior members—who would be recognized in many boardrooms around the city.

His task would not be easy. Alberta did not then have the robust economy that it enjoys now—the decrease in oil prices following the run-up of the 1970s and the arrival of the National Energy Program had put the province's main industry into the doldrums, and donation budgets were hard-pressed.

So the Sponsorship Committee started early, a year before the conference, and used a direct mail approach to solicit contributions. They developed a recognition program to ensure all donors received appropriate recognition whether they provided gifts of money, items or services. Sponsorship worked closely with those parts of conference planning that used donated services, such as printing and photocopying.

And they worked closely with the Scrounge Committee—the brainchild of Ruth Ann Yardley, a friend and colleague from the days we shared at Alberta Public Affairs. Her vision was that the conference could use a myriad of items and services and that these might be easier to get than financial support. Ruth Ann and her crew went looking for everything from items for the give-away conference grab bag to word processing services. Ultimately, the Scrounge Committee combined with the Sponsorship Committee as the conference drew near.

One of the fund-raising activities was a benefit auction for the conference. Although it raised only a bit of money, $2,800, and it took some organizing work, the relatively small audience participated with enthusiasm and bid aggressively. And it was real, tangible activity that brought a real sense of achievement to the work that was being done.

In the end, the sponsorship work was worthwhile. It raised goods, services and cash totaling $21,709. Overall, the conference showed total revenue of $93,181, expenses of $68,388 and total earnings of $24,793.

At the outset, one of our goals was to produce the "best CPRS conference ever." What we got was not perfect—our wrap-up report was half filled with "things that could be improved" and there was about the same amount of "things we did right"—but it was excellent. The program was well designed, the speakers were well chosen and well received, the operations went smoothly, attendance was good, and more money was returned to the National Society than from any previous conference. We had included many PR professionals in the organization and we felt good about what we had accomplished.

Joe Will, APR, B.Sc., grew up on a farm near Milo, Alberta, about 90 km southeast of Calgary. While completing his degree at the University of Alberta, he worked for the campus newspaper, *The Gateway*. This was followed by six years at Canadian Press, seven years with the Alberta Government Public Affairs Bureau and eight years as Director of Public Relations at Trimac Limited. He left public relations in 1989 to pursue a career in the wine industry. He has a graduate diploma in winemaking from the University of Adelaide and now is winemaker and co-owner of Strewn Winery in Niagara-on-the-Lake, Ontario.

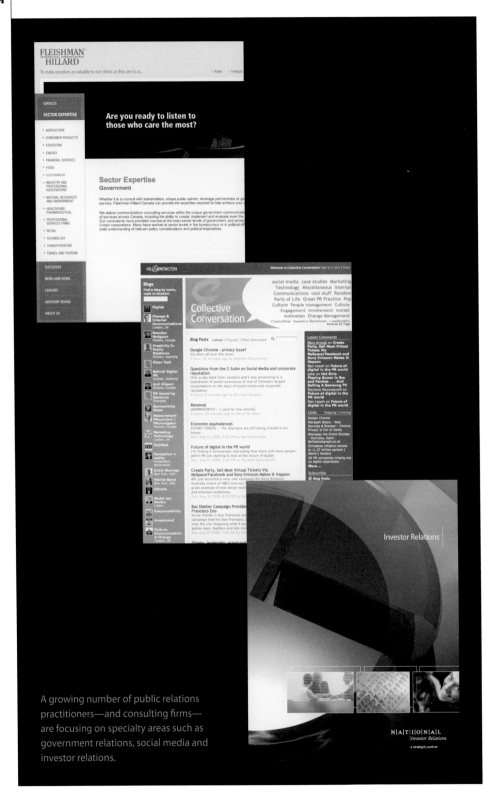

A growing number of public relations practitioners—and consulting firms— are focusing on specialty areas such as government relations, social media and investor relations.

12

The Road to Specialization:

Moving away from being generalists

By Maureen Payne, APR, FCPRS

Public relations practitioners historically have been primarily generalists. But that has changed, and today there are more and more specialists in the business, concentrating on government relations, social media, investor relations, corporate social responsibility, community investment or other emerging areas of specialization. This is an overview of three of these areas of special practice.

Introduction

The number of public relations practitioners and public relations practices in Calgary has grown considerably over the past 50 years. Calgary has been at the forefront of a number of developments as the Alberta resource economy demanded communication solutions for many issues in business and government. Today, Calgary boasts the second highest number of head offices of Fortune 500 companies in Canada, many demanding a variety of highly skilled public relations professionals.

The traditional PR firm has grown from a generalist practice to one that is now often integrated with the various marketing and communication areas. Who will ever forget the age-old question—Is advertising part of public relations? While we are all past the advertising question (due in large part to the successful PR practice of John Francis' firm, which had a strong advertising arm), the PR firm now integrates a broad range of specialties. Individual PR business boutiques also evolved in a number of key areas, most notably investor relations, marketing communication, issues management, government relations and more recently shops which focus on the "social media".

Greater knowledge of how to influence your audiences and better understanding of the attitudes and opinions of each stakeholder provided new areas of specialization for the public relations practitioner.

The tactics and tools to deliver the message also changed. No longer were communicators "channel planners". Communicators have become "stewards" of the message, according to Brendan Hodgson, Vice-President, Digital at Hill & Knowlton. The advent of the Internet, digital communication and the ongoing development of social media—Facebook, YouTube and other Internet-based tools—have added another dimension to PR. The result is a proliferation of new PR agencies (and new specialties within existing agencies) dedicated to social and digital communications.

A look at three of the major areas of specialization which grew out of the early days of public relations include the formal practice of government relations (GR), investor relations (IR), and the newest—social media and digital communications.

Government relations

Government relations is a relatively new discipline going back about 30 to 35 years in Alberta and across Canada generally. (Although one would be naïve to think that it is only in the past 30 to 35 years that governments were lobbied!) Environmentalism and greater awareness of the damages of industrialization were increasing; investigative journalism was rampant; and TIME *Magazine, The Economist* and other major publications explored the impact of environmental damage (Bhopal, Love Canal) due to lax government regulations.

Even at home, in Alberta and Calgary, we had environmental challenges. A former Imperial Oil refinery site in the southeast of the city was the signature environmental issue of the 1970s, and this same area continues to haunt Imperial as they continue to reclaim a residential site which suffered as a result of seepage of contaminated products. All of these incidents, south and north of the border, prompted federal and provincial and state governments to increase their scrutiny of industry, and influenced provincial and federal governments in Canada to act on their environmental and industrial regulations. During the same period, the oilsands were well under way, and oil and natural gas plays in the Western Sedimentary Basin continued to add to production in Alberta. In order to meet the business objectives of the growing energy industry, support from the public relations/government relations ranks was required.

The proliferation of environmental regulations made it essential for industry to have greater awareness and understanding of the impact of the regulatory environment on their business operations. The Lougheed government introduced a Department of the Environment in 1971, and increased the number of environmental regulations, while the former Energy Resources Conservation Board (ERCB), founded in Alberta in 1938, had its own conservation regulations in place.

For industry, the time was ripe for government relations, regulatory and policy development expertise.

Environmental issues were not the only impetus for the establishment of a more formal approach to government relations. The 1980s saw the emergence of a number of major transactions requiring provincial or federal regulatory policy change. The privatization of Alberta Government Telephones is an example of a major government-business transaction that required the participation of many consultants, including government relations and financial experts to steer the transaction. As a result of the AGT transactions, a government relations consultancy—GPC Canada (now Fleishman-Hillard)—was created in Alberta.

Jim Campbell, Executive Director of the Progressive Conservative Party of Alberta, a former GPC consultant and later the government relations counsel for BP Canada, has a good vision of the strengths and weaknesses of government relations in recent years. A 15-year GR veteran, Campbell sees an increasing demand for government relations expertise.

"Corporations have to tell their story to government," says Campbell, "before specific interest groups get there first. Interest groups and the proliferation of NGOs are media savvy; if industry can get the facts to government in advance, companies have a better chance of influencing decisions made on industry's behalf."

Campbell also views government relations and public relations as corporate partners in an organization. The two areas of practice "belong together in a corporation" and both sides can learn from one another's experience.

In the future, the government relations business may be influenced by its own regulatory requirements. Alberta is currently investigating a Lobbyist Act, whereby individuals working on behalf of corporations and industry associations must register (e.g. the Lobby Register) stating the nature of the business the lobbyist (or government relations consultant) is working on for the client. "What lobbyists do affects Albertans," says Campbell. "It is a legitimate activity…with major changes in the business environment, there is more acceptance of the government relations profession."

Over the years, post-secondary institutions have responded to the demand for further education in public policy training. Public Policy faculties and schools popped up throughout Canada and in Alberta. Mount Royal College introduced a public policy program in the Communications faculty in 2000, and many university Political Science faculties also have areas of study focusing on government and policy development. The University of Calgary raised the bar in 2008 when it launched the creation of a centre of expertise that focuses on public policy, headed by renowned economist Jack Mintz. The U of C program will become a national centre of research, analysis and discourse, offering mentorship for generations of bright young students. Future government relations consultants now have a place to hone their skills.

As the first decade in the 21st Century comes to a close, most of the major Alberta corporations and associations have dedicated internal and external government relations resources in place. Energy policy continues to create the greatest demand for government relations support—both internal staff and external consulting expertise—with the debate over climate change, carbon tax and royalties continuing to be high-demand areas for government relations counsel.

Many GR professionals today have government and public relations experience. Professionals such as Peter Kinnear at CNRL, Cathy Cram at ConocoPhillips and Evan Bahry with the Independent Power Producers of Alberta are currently employed on the corporate or association side, having once served in GR consultancies.

Other public relations professionals work both sides of the business—PR and GR. Pat O'Reilly, Vice-President, Communications and Public Affairs for Suncor Energy and a long-time CPRS member, now spends much of her time dedicated to the complex government issues around the oilsands industry. D'Arcy Levesque, another PR veteran at Enbridge, also dedicates a great deal of his time to the business of government and its impacts on the pipeline company.

Many companies have increased their in-house GR resources, and moved away from relying only on external consultants. However, many individual practitioners, with national and local government relations firms with in-depth policy expertise, still are in demand in Alberta.

According to some observers, including Jim Campbell, who has worked both sides of the fence, "Solo practitioners have a great deal of policy expertise and should be relied upon for counsel". Names such as Rod Love and Gord Olsen, both long-time Klein government aides, "understand how policy is made." Others such as Ken Boessenkool of Hill & Knowlton, Lorraine Royer of Global Public Affairs, and consultants with the larger PR/GR firms are highly knowledgeable and work in close harmony with their PR colleagues.

Social media

The more progressive public relations strategies today incorporate digital and/or social media. The changes which have occurred with Internet-based tools and tactics have had a profound effect on public relations practices.

In Calgary, three public relations firms that embrace social media as part of the integrated service offering include two national firms and one regional firm— NATIONAL Public Relations, Hill & Knowlton and Brookline Public Relations.

NATIONAL is taking an aggressive approach to social marketing, according to Beth Diamond, Managing Director of the Calgary office. NATIONAL's Calgary office is the leader for the firm in Canada, and the Calgary office is seeing more of their colleagues across the country adopt approaches proposed for Alberta clients.

"We are learning a lot about social marketing—how to strategically use it for message dissemination, how to determine what others are saying about a corporate entity in a world of electronic vastness, and how to determine how influential the social media environment is on an organization," says Diamond.

Shauna MacDonald, President and founder of Brookline Public Relations, a leading integrated PR agency in Calgary, says that social media bring significant opportunities to the PR industry. She notes that while some would argue social media have risen too quickly, companies of all sizes are reconsidering budgets for social media campaigns, monitoring tools and discussing techniques for client/customer engagement.

And as much as some are worried about the "loss of control", MacDonald states that social media activities—when appropriate—need to be built into strategies and plans from the beginning. "Social media principles give companies the ability to customize their communications strategies—giving audiences what they want, when they want it," she says. Moreover, social media activities also provide companies with the ability to adapt to a specific audience. With social media, engagement is no longer about a product or brand. It is about the experience and the ability to relate.

"On today's digital and wireless racetrack lined with Blackberrys, iPhones and voice communication devices, companies need tools to compete with the ever-increasing market chatter." MacDonald sees nothing but upside for companies willing to embrace social media as a key component to their communications and PR strategies.

In a July 2007 Forrester Research report entitled *B2B Marketers Dip a Toe into Emerging Tactics*, Principal Analyst Laura Ramos found that, as of the fourth quarter of 2006, only 37 per cent of B2B marketers surveyed used blogs, social networks or user-generated content in their efforts. But, says the analyst, "Wikis, forums and networks have the potential to deepen the conversation between vendors and buyers."

There is no right or wrong way to incorporate the new media, but in today's communication, digital is essential. Blogosphere, reputation aggregators, e-communities and social networks are part of the new media that public relations strategists must incorporate in their planning. Leveraging conversational online buzz to increase product anticipation and target a specific demographic is essential for some PR programs.

Some agencies now specialize in digital communication, while others believe in a more integrated approach to the practice of digital communication. Integration of digital with traditional forms of communication is prominent at Hill & Knowlton, NATIONAL and many of the other larger multinationals. Other niche firms are dedicated to digital, and make it their core business. Frequently, these same firms also provide traditional communication services including print, media relations, and other marketing services.

Hill & Knowlton speaks to the vitality of the social media as a crisis communication resource. "In keeping an integrated approach, the H&K PR practitioners have a greater influence on their client's business, as they have been introducing digital communication as part of their client's day-to-day communication plans, " says Brendan Hodgson.

"When a crisis hits, or a large campaign is introduced, it is more convenient to execute the digital portion of a program because some of the digital and social media tactics and communication methods are in place." For example, introducing a "dark site" on a company's website in the event of a crisis provides a strong proactive communication strategy for a company.

Crisis communication is a natural fit for social media. For the last 10 years, the crisis communication industry has been slowly embracing digital tools. However, not as effectively as they could, says the H&K practice leader. "Social media is changing how we communicate to our audiences during a crisis for two reasons—the environment in which our messages are being delivered and how people are using websites. With close to 75 per cent of Canadians under 40 frequenting websites, it is no wonder that there is strong consideration for the use of digital during a crisis."

The ability to speak directly with the public, customers, communities, media and other stakeholders, without a "filter", is paramount during a crisis. "The CEO speaks directly to clients, customers, regulators and other stakeholders through blogs as well as continually updating the media file. Short media updates on the website provide ongoing and new information for the media without worrying about the old fashioned deadline," says the digital leader. To successfully execute a digital crisis strategy does require the cooperation of the organization's Legal and IT departments, but "this has not been hard to do," says Hodgson.

In June 2008, Alberta Oilsands introduced a high-impact web-based strategy into their PR plan. The site was launched to begin a dialogue that several senior executives said is long overdue. Some oil industry senior statesmen will participate in the website by responding directly to questions from the public within the site's discussion forum.

NATIONAL, the agency responsible for the 2008 Alberta Oilsands strategy, encouraged the industry to include social marketing, which included messages to invite participants to dialogue on the website. "Assessment of the relationship developed between the industry and participants in the forum will form a part of the traditional research, which will be evaluated in order to help influence opinion of the larger public audiences," says Beth Diamond.

John Larsen, principal of Corpen Group, a niche consultancy dedicated to issues management and crisis/risk communication, agrees that social media are part of rapidly changing trends in how companies can conduct more effective issues management and communicate with greater impact during a crisis.

"With the proficient use of social media by key stakeholders, issues get mobilized so much more quickly," says Larsen. "The challenge for organizations is not just to stay ahead of the emerging issues, but to engage in the debate with timeliness, conviction, and truth." Larsen also points out that whether it is dealing with issue mitigation or managing through crisis, the use of social media will force practitioners to think broadly about how their communications process—information vetting, approvals, production—"will need to stay ahead of the technology curve." Although he suggests that this may be a difficult adaptation for some companies, it will ultimately prove beneficial.

Specific to social media and the application for crisis communications, Larsen says that the emerging communications tools provide PR specialists with tremendous opportunities for instant messaging and audience feedback. "In crises, we tend to default to thinking about the media, but we also need to think more consciously about our core stakeholders and our employees, and this is where social networking tools prove their worth," says Larsen. "If people have electricity they can stay connected to every development, capture new instructions, and even be part of the story for media framing the crisis." Larsen is adamant that when it comes to crisis communications and the new uses of social media, it has very literally become a paradigm shift. "We need to realize that now, to a much larger degree, we take our direction from our audiences, who demand unmediated and instant communications."

Digital and traditional communication tools work hand-in hand; it is unlikely that one would be used without the other. Furthermore, digital PR practices are not just about social media. A broad range of opportunities exist that have not been fully explored by the PR industry, and need to be.

PR practitioners must learn to embrace how a digital strategy can enhance a program. Having the ability to articulate a digital strategy is a challenge, and for the over-40 practitioner it is even more of a challenge. While social media are quite well developed, the practices are not yet instinctive.

How are PR colleges and universities keeping pace with the demands of the digital communication world? While more could be done, there is a culture shift happening. "Slowly schools are embracing the technology and educating their students on how technology enhances public relations. As many of the PR practitioners come from the journalism ranks, there is also a need for the journalism schools to be more advanced as well," says Hodgson.

Investor relations

Investor relations is another aligned communications business with roots in strategic communications. While investor relations practices have existed for some time, the integration of communication and investor relations has become more common in recent years. The major national consulting firms specialize in investor and financial communications, while a number of smaller niche firms are also prominent in Calgary.

A variety of agencies provide a broad range of strategic services in investor and financial communications. The firms integrate the disciplines of finance, communication and marketing between a public company and the investment community, in order to enable fair and effective capital markets.

In the past, the small niche firms dedicated to investor relations provided a complete roster of services for the small publicly traded company, and more specialized services for the larger companies. The larger publicly traded firms generally have their own in-house IR resources—generally a financial function, but one that works closely with PR—but at times require additional support (e.g. writing and producing the annual report, preparing for the annual meeting or drafting the script for the investor road show).

Retired investor relations consultant Jim Osborne provided investor and financial communication consulting from 1992 to 2002. The Internet provided the greatest change for Osborne during his tenure as an IR consultant.

"The Internet had a huge impact, increasing the internal corporate capacity for smaller companies," he says. No longer did the small company rely on the consultant for analyst information as information was quickly obtained through Internet access. Consultants continued to provide content and other substantive information for business plans, annual reports, road shows and other stakeholder communication needs.

Shauna MacDonald adds that investor relations and financial communications are not just key communications strategies for publicly traded companies. She advises clients that have an interest in going public and even those that don't but have an interest in building credibility and awareness to act like a public company.

"Disclosing information on a timely basis, building profile in the marketplace with media, industry analysts and financial analysts are just a few actions to create mindshare within key markets and with specific audiences," she says.

Notable in the investor relations business is Jane Savidant, founder and President of Result Communications. Result celebrated 25 years as an independent agency primarily dedicated to investor communications, including the writing and production of annual reports, websites and investor research, as well as advising the oil and gas community on other strategic investor related areas. She, too, leveraged her success by merging with Hill & Knowlton in 2006, and then managing the general H&K practice as well as overseeing the investor relations business.

Grant Howard, a former journalist and PR consultant, carved a niche for his business in the mid-1990s and now serves a broad range of energy clients on the investor side. With approximately 10 staff, including an investor analyst, writer, digital support and logistics people for road show execution, the locally owned and operated agency is one of a few Calgary boutiques dedicated to investor relations.

In summary, as the public relations discipline expands and the breadth of knowledge increases, specialization will very likely continue to increase. Communication professionals must have a strong understanding of the basic principles of public relations—research, analysis, communications and evaluation— but the move toward focusing on a single area of expertise may well be the future for new entrants to the business. Specialization undoubtedly will continue to grow.

Maureen Payne, APR, FCPRS, came to Alberta in 1972 following a short career in the news media in Halifax. She was educated at the University of Prince Edward Island (BA, 1970) and the University of Western Ontario (Diploma in Journalism, 1971). As one of the first Public Affairs Officers for the Alberta Public Affairs Bureau, she provided PR counsel and support to the various government departments and the Premier's Office in 1972/74. A move to Edmonton with the Bureau provided a career in marketing communications with Travel Alberta and the 75th Anniversary Commission. For the past 25 years she has consulted in Edmonton and Calgary, first with her own firm, and then later merging with GPC Canada. She is now an independent consultant. Her expertise includes issues management, stakeholder consultation and communication research. She was President of CPRS Calgary in 1991/92. She is a Director of the Public Relations Foundation.

Fifty years ago, news releases were hand delivered or mailed to news media. Now, with requirements for full, fair and simultaneous disclosure, companies rely on specialized news services to ensure instantaneous electronic dissemination of news releases.

13 From Teletype to Internet:

The changing face of news delivery

By Joe Vecsi

In the last 50 years, there have been many changes, none more dramatic than that of communications technology. Printing has gone from hot-lead typesetting to computer-driven printing-on-demand. Personal communication has gone from land lines to personal cell and satellite phones. One of the most dramatic changes for PR practitioners has been the technology for issuing news releases. Today, a number of companies offer state-of-the-art news delivery in Calgary, but the first organization to initiate such service here was CNW. This is a look at the changes in news delivery technology from their perspective.

In the early days, the telegraph lines that followed Canada's long-distance railway tracks were the conduit for news collection in Canada. The lines carried business and personal messages plus national, Imperial and world news and, in their way, were as busy as the tracks themselves. From the beginning, the practice of gathering and selling news could be a lucrative one.

In fact, in 1894 Canadian Pacific Railway (CPR) received a monopoly franchise in Canada to distribute the news of the mighty Associated Press (AP). CPR held the exclusive distribution rights in Canada for 16 years until a hefty price increase by the railway forced competition from Western Associated Press (WAP). Made up of three dailies in Winnipeg, WAP challenged the CPR monopoly and in 1910 won the rights to the AP feed, effectively knocking CPR out of the picture.

From WAP and similar news co-operatives in Central Canada and the Maritimes came the birth of Canadian Press (CP) in 1917. To facilitate the exchange of news across a vast and sparsely populated country, newspaper publishers created the Canadian Press during the First World War when publishers were desperate to bring news of Canadian troops in Europe to their readers. The Canadian Press began generating its own news copy and its war coverage transformed it from distributor of information to Canada's national news reporting agency.

CP built a Canadian network by signing member newspapers to support the news co-operative with membership fees. Part of CP's early financing was a $50,000 federal grant to pay for telegraph lines that would link the country from coast to coast. That funding ended in 1924 by mutual agreement. CP's founding publishers did not want to risk the appearance of compromise by accepting government money.[1]

Eventually, the concept of a non-editorial newswire service began to be discussed. The service would provide full-text news releases to the media from organizations with news to tell. So with a capital investment of $30,000 and three on staff, Canada NewsWire (now CNW Group) was born in 1960.

In the early years, CNW used teletype to send out an average 20 news releases a day. However, newsrooms were only beginning to adopt this revolutionary technology and CNW actually had to market printers to editors in order to provide newswire service. In some instances, CNW would rush couriers to businesses in order to pick up news releases for processing.

In 1982, the industry was revolutionized when CNW transmitted the first news release from a computer to a printer. The first transmission increased the speed from teletype speed of 100 words per minute to the blinding speed of 300 words per minute.[2]

Following the advent of the computer and electronic printer, the next major advance in the delivery of news came with satellite transmission in 1988. The speed of transmission and the ability to serve remote locations was vastly improved, but huge costs were involved. The industry invested millions of dollars into this technology and CNW alone spent close to half a million dollars to put the required infrastructure in place.

Sunspots were among the problems we faced, and from time to time they would cause havoc—particularly when companies needed to file earnings. Also known as solar flares, sunspots can cause disruptions in electrical utilities, satellite-based communications and cell phones and pagers. For companies who depend on sequential filing of financial data, sunspots represented a major problem as they would interfere with a satellite's transmission and throw the news release distribution process out of order.[3]

Although satellite technology proved itself for more than a decade, a major paradigm shift occurred with the advance of the Internet. For the first time, the public had direct access to newswire feeds via the Internet. "There was an initial perception that the Internet was a danger to the health of the newswire industry by opening the real-time news feeds to the average consumer," according to Melanie Kurzuk, a Senior Vice-President at CNW. "However, the driving force was public demand primarily with retail investors and corporate Canada."

CNW first began posting news releases in virtual real-time on its website in 1994. Internet users could now access news releases or search for archived releases instantly, free of charge. And the technology empowered organizations to take control of their news distribution. "The Internet not only widened the range of stakeholder groups a corporation can access, it allowed them to access these groups directly," said David Milliken, another CNW Senior Vice-President.

The introduction of this new technology also afforded the organization the opportunity to launch a range of new products and services. Customers were desperately seeking a cost-effective, one-stop solution for getting their photos to the desktops of editors. This led to the launch of CNW Photo Services, which has distributed more than 2,500 images and booked more than 450 photo assignments across Canada. More than 800 media outlets now access CNW's photo archives.

Calgary public relations practitioner Gordon McCann tells a story that illustrates how recent are the changes in photographic technology that we now all take for granted. He was on the quest for the perfect annual report shot. The year was 1998. "We were working on an annual report for a company called Neutrino Resources Inc., located in the building that housed the Alberta Stock Exchange (part of today's TSX Venture Exchange).

"My photographer, the artist and I wanted to get a shot of the two principals of the company hard at work in the late hours and in order to do this we decided to shoot from an adjacent building, Calgary Place. In today's high-tech world of photography this shot probably could have been achieved through digital imaging or superimposing one shot over another, but 10 years ago it required bribing several security guards and physically darkening all other offices surrounding the shot."

Calgary has always been at the forefront of technology in Canada, as evidenced by the popularity of webcasting and podcasting. Early adopters of webcasting in Calgary include Petro-Canada, Suncor, Boardwalk Equities and Circa Enterprises. These organizations found webcasting to be a very effective vehicle for broadcasting annual general meetings and providing a forum for interactive dialogue on quarterly earnings.

Podcasting started as a tool primarily used within the online community, to share information and build common groups of interest. It has now evolved into a widely adopted communications tool used by a wide range of corporations and government agencies. The CBC has been one of the most aggressive adopters of podcasting and they have a majority of radio shows now available for time-shifted download at the listener's convenience. All CNW client podcasts are posted in the iTunes Music Store and available on CNW's website.

So where is news delivery going? The biggest trend by far is what is being labelled as "social media," the ability of organizations to influence the massive online community through blogs, select news feeds and so on.

Most media experts agree that traditional forms of news delivery such as the newswire will always be important but smart organizations now understand the potential of social media and the online community.

In the age of 24-hour news channels, new media and consolidation, the way news is distributed continues to change rapidly. So are the expectations of the organizations providing the news. According to CNW's Joe Freeman, "We need to act as an enabler, providing a combination of traditional and non-traditional services which allow customers to reach their stakeholders directly."

In less than a century we have moved from telegraph to teletype to Internet, and from the typewriter to the word processor to the iPhone. One cannot imagine what will happen in the next 100 years.

Joe Vecsi is based in Toronto, where he is Corporate Communications Manager for CNW Group, responsible for strategic planning and event management. He has worked for a variety of organizations including FedEx, Labatt, The Movie Network and the Ontario Lottery and Gaming Corporation. He began his career working in issues management and communications planning with the Ontario Government.

The Calgary CNW experience

By Larry Cardy

I began working with Canada NewsWire during a period in which there was a rapid transformation of the technology used for news distribution. My career with CNW started in Calgary in 1975. I moved to Vancouver to set up an office five years later.

The newswire technology of the day was public telex and teletype. CNW's private teletype network comprised about 25 major newspapers and news-gathering agencies across the country. This was supplemented by telex and courier delivery to other key national/local news and financial media.

I was selected for the job at CNW because of my telex/teletype experience and ability to read the perforated, five-level, hole-punched tape that spewed out when you typed a news release into a tape machine. The only way you could proof the news release copy for errors was to read the holes in the paper tape—a skill I'd picked up in the military.

When I joined CNW, many organizations, including public companies, were still delivering their news releases via mail and courier. CNW was still a young company and had only recently established a presence in Alberta. In the beginning, it took a substantial effort to convince these "old-school" PR people to move away from their one-on-one telephone, mail and courier system to CNW's state-of-the-art, same-day delivery, news release wire service.

On average, a one-page news release would take about one hour to type on to the "tape machine" and proof for errors before it was fed through our tape reader on to the CNW teletype network. We would then "dial-up" the other news outlets, one at a time, through regular telephone and feed them copy on the three telex machines. If the gods were with us and we had no mechanical problems or busy telephone lines, we would get a one-page news release out to key media in the blinding speed of one to two hours.

In 1977, CNW Calgary was one of the few companies in Calgary to install a fax machine. This machine was the size of a small fridge. A single-page news release was wrapped around a large drum. You would then dial up the phone number of the receiving fax machine, hear a connection and press the send button. The drum would start to turn slowly and a "stylus" would slowly move down the page on the drum. If the stars were aligned properly and the machine did not stop turning (which it did frequently) and you kept your telephone connection, then your news release would magically appear on the receiving fax machine in 20 to 30 minutes.

The biggest change at Canada NewsWire, though, came when we "computerized" our networks in the early 1980s. This was probably the most important event in the organization's history. To run our wire service software and save news release copy, we all received XT computers. The latest technology, these little machines didn't even have hard drives. Instead, they had floppy drives, which used flexible ("floppy") discs with negligible storage capacity by today's standards. Those discs quickly accumulated, and filing them all presented challenges.

It was a major undertaking in 1980 to approach the news media on our teletype network and replace the 60-word-per-minute teletype machines with 100-word-per-minute "dot matrix" printers—at the time, an unheard-of speed.

In the mid-1970s, we had about 30 clients in all of Western Canada, primarily Calgary-based oil companies. Our Prairie Region business developed rapidly throughout the mid-to-late-1970s due to the rapid growth of the oilpatch. The oil companies were rapidly accepting CNW's technology as the preferred methodology for prompt access to the media. In addition, virtually all the oilpatch PR people were active members of the CPRS Calgary chapter during my tenure from 1975 to 1980.

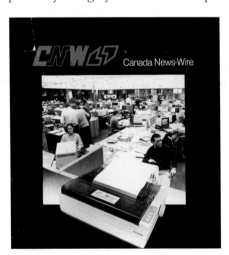

The 1980s saw CNW switch from teletype machines to faster "dot matrix" printers.

PR people who I remember that were active in the oilpatch in the 1970s were folks like Tom Johnson of ATCO, Dave McAsey, Dave Annesley and the two Jim Rennies, senior and junior. The dominant PR firm in Calgary in the 1970s was Francis, Williams & Johnson, and John Francis was a strong influence in the CPRS Calgary chapter, which was one of the fastest-growing chapters during this time.

The oil industry takeover and merger frenzy in the late 1970s resulted in many occasions when CNW was working for two or three companies involved in a hostile takeover battle. It became very tense and a major exercise in diplomacy when we would literally have two or three PR people in our Calgary office at the same time wanting their release to move on the wire before their competitors' copy.

CNW Calgary grew rapidly during the oil boom in the mid-to-late-1970s. Other industries, as well as unions, associations and governments in the Prairie Region and British Columbia, started to see the benefit of using CNW to deliver their news promptly to the media and financial community. In five short years, the Calgary office grew to a team of eight individuals with a client base made up of most of the major oil industry companies and many non-corporate organizations. There were several months in the late 1970s when revenue at the Calgary office—then a city of less than half a million—surpassed that of CNW Toronto and Montréal. Our business was also starting to build in other provinces as word spread that CNW was the best way to get your news in front of the media.

Larry Cardy had a seven-year stint in the communications branch of the Canadian Armed Forces (Air Force) before joining Canada NewsWire in 1975. He managed the organization's Western operations out of Calgary from 1975 to 1980 before moving to Vancouver to establish an office. He retired from CNW as Vice-President, Western Canada in 2007.

Public consultation for an Enbridge pipeline
project provides an opportunity for the
company to provide information about its
proposed project, and an opportunity for
landowners and other stakeholders to examine
proposed route maps, ask questions, voice their
concerns and provide input to the project.

14

The Evolution
of Public Consultation:

From the back door to the front porch

By Alan Roth, APR and Doug Ford, APR

Public consultation is another area of specialization for public relations practitioners, one that goes to the heart of what public relations aspires to be all about—two-way communication that builds relationships with key publics. It is a specialty that has been embraced by many organizations, and is, in fact, a requirement for any resource development project that seeks regulatory approval. This chapter looks at the evolution of public consultation in Alberta.

In the beginning, public relations was essentially media relations and press agentry. But as public relations evolved and matured, its primary focus became building reputation and recognition from a branding and marketing perspective. However, with economic growth and the advent of greater concern about the environment, affected publics began demanding more involvement in civic and business decision-making. One result was that PR practice areas like government relations, issues management—and public consultation—began to come into their own.

While other professionals, including municipal planners, engineers and biologists, sometimes found themselves involved in managing public consultations, the key to successful consultation is an understanding of and expertise in communication. So it was no surprise that the same individuals who pioneered modern public relations in Calgary were also directly involved in fostering the practice and professionalization of public consultation in Alberta. CPRS and its Calgary chapter members have played a critical role in this development over the past five decades.

The path leading to the present state of public consultation has been one of dramatic change, challenges and growth. Engagement practices considered to be the norm today simply didn't exist prior to the 1990s. The stakeholder's role was undefined, and landowners typically had little or no influence over resource development projects in their area.

The role of public consultation has been particularly vital in Alberta, where resource development has become more and more difficult and faces growing unpopularity. The fragile state of relations between industry and the public today would baffle practitioners of just 15 or 20 years ago—let alone those of 50 years ago. Factors such as increasing energy prices, widespread climate change fears, well-funded and well-organized environmentalists, and a well-informed and engaged public have created a "perfect storm" for both the oil and gas industry as well as the electrical power industry.

This amounts to a tectonic shift from the *status quo* in the late 1950s. At that time, Alberta resource development companies rather took for granted landowners' consent when surface land use rights were required for drilling wells or building pipelines and other related facilities. In the days of Buddy Holly, bobby socks and Blue Flame Kitchens, granting energy companies access to private land was almost seen as a patriotic duty. Energy infrastructure was still relatively new and almost universally welcomed. Prairie province dwellers also shared North America's infatuation with those big, shiny, gas-guzzling automobiles when pump prices were no obstacle. Greenhouse gases were unheard of, and only the very worldly were aware of a phenomenon then known as "smog". Given that much of the population of the day could still recall coal-burning furnaces, wood stoves, ice-boxes, kerosene lamps and freezing dashes to the "outdoor plumbing" in winter, it's no surprise that the conveniences made possible by oil and gas and electrical transmission were well-received.

Of course, as governments, regulators, agencies and stakeholder expectations changed, so too did the strategies and tactics consultation specialists proposed. In fact, the regulatory process has played a significant role in driving present-day public consultation. Whether it was urban or rural infrastructure development, the seeds of consultation were planted by those organizations that required some form of stakeholder consent to move projects forward. This meant that Alberta's first public consultation practitioners were often land agents whose primary role was to negotiate access to private lands to facilitate infrastructure development. For years, land agents were often the first (and only) face of oil and gas companies for stakeholders throughout the province.

During those early years, public consultation was a sub-set of general project notification for public relations practitioners. Regulatory expectations at the federal, provincial and municipal levels were initially designed to ensure stakeholders were notified about impending project applications, though often just barely before the trucks and equipment arrived. Notification not infrequently meant a letter followed promptly by a stream of workers and materials.

However, by the 1970s, change was in the air in Alberta—politically, socially and industrially. The first substantial energy boom transformed the whole concept of consultation practices for industry. Cursory telephone calls became in-person meetings, which evolved into public meetings and community forums, such as open houses. Letters became introductions to bulletins. Bulletins began to evolve into colour brochures and detailed maps and drawings. Brochures formed the backbone of display panels. Display panels led to videos. Before long, extensive communications materials and public forums became the norm—not the exception—when engaging with affected stakeholders.

Not that many years ago "consultation" might mean an annual visit and sending out the annual corporate calendar or fridge magnet to landowners. Today's toolbox is much more sophisticated.

It includes reviewing and understanding the broad social and political environments surrounding the project, the development of strategic plans, analysis of issues, identification of stakeholder audiences, and the creation and use of a variety of communications tools. It involves one-on-one contacts with landowners and other stakeholders; developing good working relationships with local news media and community leaders; and use of open houses or similar forums to give all local stakeholders an opportunity to meet with project proponents, gather information, ask questions and share their ideas and concerns. It can include traditional communications media such as brochures, ads in local newspapers and mailouts; and it can include broadcast emails and websites—online tools that provide information, and the opportunity to respond, ask questions and offer input.

Of course the use of any or all of these tools assumes a thorough knowledge of the regulatory requirements for the project that is being advanced, a broad range of public relations knowledge and expertise, and the capability for database management of the many components of the stakeholder engagement programs.

In 2008, virtually no resource development is possible without first consulting those who are or may be affected in some way. The Government of Canada's Regulatory Policy, for example, requires that federal departments and agencies demonstrate that Canadians have been consulted and that they have had an opportunity to participate in developing or modifying regulations and regulatory programs. Similar policies exist at provincial and municipal levels of government.

Now, the most rustic-seeming agriculturist may be extremely aware of— and articulate about—his or her rights (due in part to good coaching by legal counsel) and regulators continue to raise the bar for public and Aboriginal consultation requirements.

A major benefit of an open house is that it provides an opportunity for employees of the project proponent—such as Enbridge's Michele Perret *(left)*—and individual stakeholders to open up a constructive and ongoing dialogue to exchange information and ideas.

In spite of ever-greater and more interactive public consultation, to read the business press is to form the impression that the oil and gas industry is under siege. The pendulum has swung far from the time when resource development and energy infrastructure were welcomed with open arms. Acronyms have been coined that characterize the current public attitude, such as NIMBY and BANANA (Not In My Back Yard and Build Absolutely Nothing Anywhere Near Anyone), together with the less well-known "CAVE" people—Citizens Against Virtually Everything.

The energy industry has never fared well in public opinion polls, with polls done 50 and more years ago reflecting the public's lack of confidence. With the growth of a NIMBY and BANANA culture, the industry continues to fare badly.

For example, a 2007 public opinion survey conducted in Canada by a large international oil and gas company found that, with one exception, oil and gas ranked lower in public esteem than all the other sectors the study covered. The exception? Only the tobacco industry was seen as less trustworthy. Even bankers and lawyers—longstanding pariahs of public opinion research—were ranked above the petroleum sector by the survey's respondents. The old adage of "what is good for industry is good for us" has been replaced with "development if necessary but not necessarily development."

Perhaps it's to be expected that the resource sector is typecast as the villain in a time as preoccupied as we are about climate change calamity and energy prices. That is a reality that energy companies are working hard to address, both in their actions to improve environmental performance and in their public communications. Consequently, in the meantime the practice of public consultation (also known by terms such as public involvement, public participation and stakeholder engagement) operates at a public-industry interface that is extremely dynamic and challenging.

In fact, together with public safety and care for the environment, it is probably fair to say that a "culture of consultation" is now the dominant ethos of resource development in Western Canada. Regardless of which term is used, all the regulators' guidelines and directives have firmly entrenched landowner and stakeholder consultation and notification requirements, with regulatory scope broadened and degrees of prescriptiveness jacked up on a regular basis.

In an age of a less deferential and more educated and sceptical citizenry, energy development regulators have learned that the public consultation component of the regulatory process must be given significantly greater attention than in the past. As a result, the National Energy Board defines a key part of its role as being "committed to ensuring that stakeholders are effectively engaged in the Board's public processes. These processes are designed so that decision-makers are presented with the complete range of views required to make fully-informed decisions in the Canadian public interest." That mandate includes public participation in public hearings, consultation with landowners, and consultation with Aboriginal peoples.

And as National Energy Board Chair and Chief Executive Gaetan Caron recently told a utility regulators conference, utility and resource development regulation is getting harder and harder. "It is a fact that public hearings about energy projects are growing in intensity and complexity. Society is evolving, people are better connected, better informed and better organized", stated Caron.

As a result, stakeholders are often not content with the kinds of public involvement opportunities currently provided, and they look for more frequent and

---

Principles of Public Consultation

Communica Public Affairs has a set of clearly defined principles that help frame its approach to the public consultation process. These principles include the following:

- We believe strongly in the value and fairness of a sincere, open and transparent stakeholder engagement process that seeks the input of those potentially affected by a decision.
- Stakeholder engagement establishes a meaningful opportunity for stakeholders to participate in arriving at decisions that, as far as possible, reflect their interests and concerns.
- Stakeholder engagement leads to better decisions and requires clear communication in an atmosphere of mutual respect and trust.
- Appropriate, effective stakeholder engagement enables a project proponent to explain goals and plans, while creating a valuable opportunity to learn more about stakeholders' views and explore how they might be incorporated into business planning.

---

meaningful ways to be involved in shaping decisions of many kinds—including decisions about resource and associated energy infrastructure developments. As well, technology is raising expectations for immediate access to reliable information and facilitating grassroots organizing and networking across groups outside of geographical boundaries and existing processes. This is directly indicated in the emergence of highly sophisticated and influential synergy groups across the province.

In our practice, we often assist proponents in designing and implementing their stakeholder consultations and communications programs. However well-crafted the communication materials and cogent the project information and messaging though, people's respect, trust and confidence must be won the old-fashioned way: by listening carefully to and taking a sincere interest in their views, fully honouring promises and commitments in a timely way, openness and transparency in all things, being accountable and, above all, by never forgetting the golden rule our parents drilled into each of us, "do unto others …."

Participating in respectful, well-organized consultation processes is a rewarding experience where barriers to productive dialogue, if not removed, are often lowered. One of the most basic tenets of public consultation is that better results are achieved when those most affected are included in the decision-making process. The process helps create legitimacy and sustainability. The alternative to engaging the public will not be an unengaged public, but a public with its own agenda and an understandable hostility to decision-making processes that appear to ignore them.

But public consultation is no magic wand, and even a well designed and implemented program of stakeholder engagement is no guarantee that opposition to a project can be overcome.

This is why organizations such as CPRS, together with others such as the International Association of Public Participation, play an increasingly important role in Canada. Public consultation is now a core element of project development. There is scarcely a hockey rink, gas field, highway interchange or oilsands project that won't have a sophisticated element of public consultation. The pioneers of the practice played a vital role in ensuring a solid foundation was established to lead us into the next half century, where public consultation is sure to be front and centre.

Alan Roth, APR, MCS, is a founder of and a partner in Communica Public Affairs Inc., a Calgary consultancy whose core business is public consultation. He has 25 years of experience in communications, 15 of that in corporate communications, public affairs and public engagement. His professional focus areas include strategic planning and implementation for stakeholder relations programs, public issues identification, public consultation, corporate communications, risk communications, crisis communications and media relations.

Doug Ford, APR, is a founder of and a partner in Communica Public Affairs Inc. He has more than 25 years of experience, and has planned, developed and implemented numerous successful public consultation programs for many of Canada's largest companies. He has extensive Alberta and B.C. regulatory experience, has served as an expert witness before the Quebec Court of Appeals, and has participated as an expert witness with respect to public consultation and communications at two National Energy Board hearings.

Epilogue

Nancy Arab

May you live in interesting times.

This is thought to be a Chinese proverb, but has also been described in some sources as a curse. I am not sure it really is a curse. Public relations is a business that thrives on "interesting times". Whether it's crisis communications, media relations, internal communications, or any facet of what we do every day, we really do live in interesting times.

The profession is said to have started with Edward L. Bernays, the Father of Public Relations. Bernays was one of the first practitioners to influence public perception, something we still do today.

I had the privilege of meeting Bernays in 1991 and spending some time with him at the IPRA World Congress. Still sharp and focused on his life-long profession, Bernays shared his insights and experiences. He certainly lived through interesting times.

Over the course of his life (he died in 1995 at 103), he saw a shift in what we define as our tenets of the profession, and the work we did. He believed strongly in education and the professional public relations practitioner. He spent much of his career trying to have public relations licensed, which in his mind would elevate it from a vocation to the level of a profession. In his address to the IPRA Congress, he again reiterated his concern that "Anyone can hang up a shingle and become a legitimate public relations practitioner."

CPRS has spent much of its 60-year history in Canada, and certainly our 50-year history in Calgary, working towards a similar goal. CPRS has always been a resource and a place for people practicing in public relations to share issues and challenges, and to share ideas. Accreditation is now a key benefit of being a CPRS member; a way to demonstrate your commitment to learning, the profession, and your own development. And Calgary has 46 accredited members.

Over the past 100 years, we've seen incredible advances in science and the development of countless new inventions. Today, advanced electronic technologies play important roles in our everyday lives. The tools we use in our business have also changed. We've gone from handwritten letters to telex to fax, and now email and Facebook. From the introduction of the telephone to cell phones and text messaging. And all these advances have changed the way we do our business.

But some things are also still the same. The benefit of the personal, one-to-one relationship is still key to building trust and reputation. Truth, honesty, and ethics still remain a strong part of our foundation, and our own reputations and standing as professionals.

The next 50 years will likely see even more changes and advances. But what will remain the same is how we represent our profession and those we represent. Ethics will always be an important part of how we act and react in the profession. Professionalism, whether through accreditation, professional recognition that comes from local or national awards, or education will remain an essential factor in the reputation and further enhancement of our work and our own standing.

And most importantly, it's the contributions that we make ourselves to the profession that help it grow and develop. When you volunteer with the society, attend a professional development event, or become accredited, you are making a personal commitment to the profession and your place in it.

I want to thank all of those who have helped make this, our 50th year in Calgary, a great celebration and recognition of our past 50 years. This book would not have been possible without the commitment of each and every volunteer. The 50th Anniversary Committee, chaired by Henry Stevens, APR, has done a wonderful job of giving us great mementos (like this written collection of 50 years of memories) and events to commemorate this year in our history.

As we move to our next 50 years, I encourage you to look at where we've arrived as a profession. This book is filled with insightful and interesting recollections from practitioners who have built our profession in Calgary. People who have blazed a trail for the rest of us to follow. People who have helped change and develop the business as it is today. People who will take us into the future.

And in using the new technology at our disposal these days, I found another proverb (or curse) to go with *May you live in interesting times.*

May you find what you are looking for.

Nancy H. Arab, APR, ABC, FCPRS
President, CPRS Calgary

Appendix: CPRS Calgary Presidents

1957/58: Tom Steele

1958/59: Ken Ford

1959/60: Jim Rennie, Sr.

1960/61: Jack Fleming

1961/62: David Wood, APR

1962/63: Lorne Frame

1963/64: John Thorburn

1964/65: John Francis, APR, FCPRS(H)

1965/66: Lloyd White

1966/67: Brock Hammond

1967/68: Alex Jupp

1968/69: Bill Speerstra

1969/70: Art Merkel

1970/71: Gordon Wemp

1971/72: Brian Somerville

1972/73: Gene Zadvorny, APR

1973/74: John Neinhuis, APR

1974: Cliff Pilkey, APR

1974/76: Cynthia Balfour, APR

1976/77: David McAsey, APR, FCPRS(H)

1977/78: Leo Van Vugt, APR

1978/79: T.A.G. Watson, APR

1979/80: Jim Rennie, Jr., APR

1980/81: Bill Watson, APR

1981/82: Jean Andryiszyn, APR

1982/83: Peter McKenzie-Brown, APR

1983/84: Janet Willson, APR

1984/85: Don Boynton, APR

1985/86: Jan Goodwin

1986/87: Joe Will, APR

1987/88: David Annesley, APR

1988/89: Merry Chellas, APR

1989/90: Ruth Ann Yardley

1990/91: Judi Gunter, APR

1991/92: Maureen Payne, APR, FCPRS

1992/93: Scott Ranson

1993/94: Presidential Coaching Team: Darlene Krusel-Hyde, APR Kent O'Connor, APR

1994/95: Sherri G. Dutton

1995/96: Shari Gallant

1996/97: Janice Robertson, APR

1997/99: Lisa Homer, APR

1999/00: Judi Gunter, APR

2000/01 Colleen Killingsworth, APR

2001/03: Shawn Kelly, APR

2003/04: Mona Gauvreau, APR

2004/05: Henry Stevens, APR

2005/06: Bonnie Elgie, APR

2006/07: Richard Truscott, APR

2007/09: Nancy Arab, APR, FCPRS

Notes

Chapter Three: Centre of a Storm

1   *Peter McKenzie-Brown, Gordon Jaremko, David Finch, The Great Oil Age: The Petroleum Industry in Canada (Calgary: Detselig Publishers, 1993), pp. 136-141.*

2   *Interview with Jack Gorman, May 23, 2008.*

3   *Interview with Hans Maciej, June 3, 2008.*

4   *Interview with Jack Gorman, op. cit.*

5   *Interview with Hans Maciej, June 3, 2008.*

6   *Department of Energy, The National Energy Programme (Ottawa: Queen's Printer, 1980).*

7   *McKenzie-Brown et al., op. cit., p. 140.*

8   *Interview with Ian Smyth, June 3, 2008.*

9   *Interview with Jack Gorman, op. cit.*

10   *Interview with Norm Elliott, May 29, 2008.*

11   *Interview with Ian Smyth, op. cit.*

12   *Interview with Hans Maciej, op. cit.*

13   *Berger et al., Northern Frontier, Northern Homeland (Ottawa: Queen's Printer, 1977).*

14   *Interview with Ian Smyth, op. cit.*

Chapter Four: Working for Big Oil

1   *Interview with Frank Dabbs, June 9 2008.*

2   *Peter Foster, Other People's Money, p 91.*

3   *Ibid., p. 92.*

4   *Ibid.*

Chapter Eight: Town Meets Gown

1   *Peter Wright, "What is a Profession," 29 Canadian Bar Review 748, 752 (1951).*

Chapter Ten: Breaking into Public Relations

1   *PR Tactics, June 2008, p. 7.*

Chapter Thirteen: From Teletype to Internet

1   *Melanie Kurzuk, "100 years of Newswires in Canada," Press Review.*

2   *Ibid.*

3   *Ibid.*

Index